WHY CAN'T THIS TEAM JUST FIND A QUARTER-BACK?

AND OTHER THOUGHTS ON LIFE IN BROWNS TOWN

Also by Terry Pluto

ON SPORTS:

Vintage Browns
Vintage Cavs
The Browns Blues
The Comeback: LeBron, the Cavs and Cleveland
Glory Days in Tribe Town (with Tom Hamilton)
Joe Tait: It's Been a Real Ball (with Joe Tait)
Things I've Learned from Watching the Browns
LeBron James: The Making of an MVP (with Brian Windhorst)
The Franchise (with Brian Windhorst)
Dealing: The Cleveland Indians' New Ballgame
False Start: How the New Browns Were Set Up to Fail
The View from Pluto
Unguarded (with Lenny Wilkens)
Our Tribe
Browns Town 1964
Burying the Curse
The Curse of Rocky Colavito
Falling from Grace
Tall Tales
Loose Balls
Bull Session (with Johnny Kerr)
Tark (with Jerry Tarkanian)
Forty-Eight Minutes, a Night in the Life of the NBA (with Bob Ryan)
Sixty-One (with Tony Kubek)
You Could Argue But You'd Be Wrong (with Pete Franklin)
Weaver on Strategy (with Earl Weaver)
The Earl of Baltimore
Super Joe (with Joe Charboneau and Burt Graeff)
The Greatest Summer

ON FAITH AND OTHER TOPICS:

The Guy with the Sign
Faith and You
Faith and You, Volume 2
Everyday Faith
Champions for Life: The Power of a Father's Blessing (with Bill Glass)
Crime: Our Second Vietnam (with Bill Glass)

WHY CAN'T THIS TEAM JUST FIND A QUARTER-BACK?

AND OTHER THOUGHTS ON LIFE IN BROWNS TOWN

TERRY PLUTO

GRAY & COMPANY, PUBLISHERS
CLEVELAND

Gray & Company, Publishers
www.grayco.com

ISBN 978-1-59851-151-2
Printed in the United States of America
1

In memory of Jim Donovan:
If only the Browns did their job
as well as he did.

CONTENTS

Why Can't This Team Just Find a Quarterback? 1
A Big Swing and Miss: Deshaun Watson 7
Al Lerner—Gone Too Soon 16
Wrong Time, Wrong Team: Tim Couch 30
The Voice of the Browns: Jim Donovan 43
Johnny Manziel—Seriously? 56
Searching and Searching: The Draft 72
No One Will Thank Sashi Brown, but They Should 79
Analytics: On and Off and On Again 83
They Got One Right: Picking Myles Garrett 92
The Hype Machine and Odell Beckham Jr. 99
Here We Go Again: Great Expectations 111
How It All Fell Apart: Baker and OBJ 119
The Odyssey of Deshaun Watson 131
She Has the Browns' Number: One Fan's Story 136
Biggest Deal Ever: Deshaun Watson Comes to Cleveland 142
One of the Great "What Ifs?": Baker Mayfield 155
The Best Since Jim Brown: Nick Chubb 164
Jim Donovan's Long Battle with Cancer 179
Quarterbacks. Again. 190
Why the Browns? 197
Acknowledgments 207

WHY CAN'T THIS TEAM JUST FIND A QUARTER-BACK?

AND OTHER THOUGHTS ON

LIFE IN BROWNS TOWN

Joshua Gunter / cleveland.com

WHY CAN'T THIS TEAM JUST FIND A QUARTERBACK?

"You gotta write another Browns book!"

I've heard that several times in the last few years.

Once again, Browns fans are frustrated, angry and downright dumbfounded by their favorite team.

When voicing their concerns to me, readers often said these two words . . . Deshaun Watson.

How could the Browns make the Deshaun Watson trade?

When it comes to moves made by the Browns, I've heard fans scream obscenities, pound tables and swear off their allegiance—for about the hundredth time.

But never tears.

Not until Deshaun Watson.

There were real tears from women who love the Browns and could not believe their team brought in the quarterback with so much ugly off-field baggage from his alleged misconduct with massage therapists. While Watson was never charged criminally, he did settle 23 civil lawsuits. He also was suspended 11 games by the NFL and fined $5 million.

The publicity was awful not only for Watson and the Browns, but for those who love the team.

The franchise must have considered the possible catastrophic consequences if the mega-trade and the fully guaranteed $230 million mega-contract failed to produce a big winner. They were real and clear—and apparently disregarded.

Many fans had their hearts broken by this move even before Watson took a snap while wearing an orange helmet. Not the kind of football heartbreak that comes from Red Right 88 or The Fumble or The Drive or the other excruciating playoff losses. This was deeper, sadder—and something that might easily have been avoided because it didn't happen on the field. It was a premeditated, ill-advised and destructive decision that is still hard to comprehend by many who love this team.

Susan Frollo sent me this email:

> When the Browns left, I was distraught. I still remember our pastor talking about it in a sermon: "We said, 'Go Browns'—and they did." Since the Browns came back, it's been a challenge to get behind them, but I've never given up on them—until the Watson trade. I still watch, but the team feels tarnished. A slap in the face to those players with such loyalty to the team and the game.

There were many more like that—hundreds over the last few years.

Cheryl Hughley sent me this:

> I have sworn off the team only once. It had nothing to do with the losing record. I could no longer root for a Deshaun Watson-led team . . . Why would any owner bring in a quarterback who essentially broke a contract with one team by refusing to play, had more than 20 pending lawsuits and had already crossed your team off his list of desirable locations?

This from Holly Monte:

> When the Browns acquired Deshaun Watson, I felt sick. Disgusted. I stopped following the Browns on social media and stopped watching the games.

From Nancy Sommer:

> Why were they so stupid to guarantee all the money? Why give away all those picks? Hard to believe, but a bigger mess than Johnny Manziel.

While the Watson deal sparked the fire for this book, this is not a book about Watson. It looks at a broader question: Why can't the Browns ever seem to get it right? Trades, draft picks, head coaches, injuries . . . Why do things so often go so wrong for this franchise? Maybe not always . . . but it sure seems that way after 25 years.

And that leads to an even bigger question . . .

Why the Browns?

Why do so many fans absolutely, positively love the Browns?

Still.

Winning? That can't be the reason. Since 1999, no NFL team has been worse than the Browns.

The Browns have not had back-to-back winning seasons since 1986–90. That was the Bernie Kosar Era, the old Browns. Remember, we're not talking about playoff seasons . . . just two seasons in a row of winning more games than they lost.

It's even worse than all the losing . . . worse than never getting to a Super Bowl, which was born in 1967.

What is worse than all that?

The team moved. The franchise walked out. Left town . . . for Baltimore.

So the Browns lose. They move. They come back. They lose some more. They draft Johnny Manziel. They actually traded up in the draft to pick Manziel in 2014.

Why?

Browns owner Jimmy Haslam said "a homeless guy" told him to pick the barely 6-foot quarterback from Texas A&M. Haslam was joking . . . I think.

But I do know that Joe Banner, before he was fired as the team's CEO, had taken Manziel off the team's 2014 draft board. Banner told me that the Browns knew all about Manziel's problems with alcohol and drugs.

"I was watching the draft, and I almost fell off the couch when the Browns picked him," Banner said.

Covering the draft, I kept thinking, "Why do the Browns keep doing stuff like this?"

In my heart, I knew the answer. It's because they're . . . well . . . *the Browns!*

If you follow the Browns, you invariably ask yourself, "Where is our quarterback?" Forty different quarterbacks since 1999 with more to come in 2025. Yet, the question lingers for fans, "Where's our quarterback?"

Manziel was a disaster. Barely played in the NFL, 14 games in two seasons. Check that, he sometimes didn't know the plays when he was on the field for the Browns. Several of the team's linemen told me that.

Sigh.

The Browns . . .

For a while, fans have been asking me to write a sequel to my book *Browns Blues* (which was itself a sequel to *False Start: How the New Browns Were Set Up to Fail*). They believed the decision to trade for and sign Deshaun Watson in 2022 was worthy of a book itself. Yes, I will deal with the Watson acquisition later in this book. But it's not the focus.

There have been bright moments. One of my favorites was how the Browns in 2020 led by Baker Mayfield made the playoffs and knocked off Pittsburgh in the first round. That was during the

John Kuntz / cleveland.com

dismal days of COVID-19 when games were played in nearly empty stadiums. But they were on TV and supplied a wonderful diversion from real life for Browns fans.

In 2023, Joe Flacco came to town seemingly out of nowhere. He started five late regular season games for the Browns, winning four. The Browns made the playoffs. He was The Associated Press NFL Comeback Player of the Year.

Now and then, good things do happen with the Browns.

Another event that inspired this book was the death of Jimmy Donovan.

The Browns' radio voice since 1999 had been battling leukemia and other forms of cancer since 2000. I wrote a three-part series about Jimmy in 2022 for The Plain Dealer and cleveland.com. After a long period of remission, his cancer returned. At that point, melanoma had attacked him. He asked me not to put that in my stories. I honored the request because Jimmy was such a great guy and was so open about his other battles with cancer. I interviewed Jimmy several other times after that series before his death on Oct. 26 2024.

Jimmy Donovan is an antidote for the Deshaun Watson mess. A Bostonian at birth, a Boston Bruins hockey fan growing up,

Donovan became the radio play-by-play voice of the Browns when the team returned in 1999 after a three-year absence.

Fans still miss him. I do, too.

Finally, I wanted to write about what it's been like for fans living in Browns Town since the team returned in 1999, with this eternal question hanging over them . . .

Why can't this team just find a quarterback?

A BIG SWING AND MISS: DESHAUN WATSON

Most Browns fans know what happened with Deshaun Watson in Cleveland.

It was a disaster off the field in terms of the negative publicity the franchise received. On the field, let's put it this way: Watson settled more civil lawsuits (23) than he started games for the Browns (19) between 2022 and 2024.

The Browns had a 9-10 record in games started by Watson. ESPN keeps a statistic, QBR, that rates quarterbacks on all play types. From 2022 to 2024 only Tennessee's Will Levis had a lower rating than Watson. The Browns kept waiting for the Deshaun Watson of Houston to show up on the field. Watson's first four NFL seasons (2017–2020, all with Houston) were a different story. The only quarterback with a higher rating after his first four years is Kansas City's Patrick Mahomes.

I had people from the Browns tell me that when they made the deal for Watson they rated him among the NFL's top three quarterbacks. At worst, they believed he'd be in the top five.

It's easy to imagine the Browns staring at videos of Watson in his best days in Houston. I'll argue Watson was a very good quarterback in Houston, but not a great one. But "very good" would have been a massive improvement over nearly all Cleveland quarterbacks since Bernie Kosar (1985–93).

So what happened?

The Browns ignored the fact Watson sat out in 2021 with a trade demand . . . and then the first batch of civil suits hit him. The Browns probably thought, *Missing a season isn't unusual. Guys sit out a year due to injuries. He'll be fine. Besides, he's only 27. He's just approaching his best seasons.*

The thinking was flawed. There was nothing ordinary about the Watson situation. The Browns and Watson were being publicly vilified due to the civil lawsuits and the unsavory stories about Watson's alleged actions with multiple female massage therapists.

Then there was the NFL disciplinary process.

I was told the Browns believed Watson would receive no more than a six-game suspension to open the 2022 season. They based that on suspensions given by the NFL to other players for off-field indiscretions. That projection was right . . . originally. An arbitrator appointed by the NFL indeed suspended Watson for six games. But there was such a public uproar, and even many people working for the NFL believed the suspension was too soft. That led to a negotiation between the NFL and the NFL Players Association. The six-game suspension became 11 games. Watson also was fined $5 million.

Later, Watson continued to say he did nothing wrong.

"I'll continue to stand on my innocence," he said at a press conference. "Just because . . . you know . . . settlements . . . and things like that happen . . . [It] doesn't mean that a person is guilty for anything. I feel like a person has an opportunity to stand on his innocence and prove that. We proved that on the legal side, and just going to continue to push forward as an individual and as a person."

Watson was talking about how he was not criminally charged. But his comment infuriated a large part of the media and fan base.

If he's innocent, why settle all the cases? Of course, the Browns wanted those cases to go away (as did the NFL) so Watson could return to the field.

The Houston Texans ended up settling civil suits with 30 women who had accused Watson's former team of "enabling Watson's behavior," according to attorney Tony Buzbee. He brought all the suits against Watson and Houston.

The Texans put out this statement:

> We were shocked and deeply saddened when we first learned of the allegations against our then franchise quarterback in March 2021. Although our organization did not have any knowledge of Deshaun Watson's alleged misconduct, we have intentionally chosen to resolve this matter amicably. This is not an admission of any wrongdoing, but instead a clear stand against any form of sexual assault and misconduct.

For Browns fans, this was one emotional gut punch after another.

I remember talking to a veteran NFL public relations director from another team (not the Browns) about Watson. He asked if anyone in the media ever did a one-on-one interview with Watson. The Browns never allowed it. Whenever Watson talked, it was in a controlled general press conference.

"That's really tough for the team," said the P.R. man. "The quarterback is the face of the franchise. You want him out there. But you don't want him being asked about the lawsuits and all that."

* * *

One clear verdict against the Watson deal was what happened when he was on the field.

When you add Watson sitting out the 2021 season in Houston plus the 11-game suspension to open the 2022 season in Cleveland, it was 700 days between regular NFL games. When he did return,

It was a huge contract, and the Browns were expecting a big return. Deshaun Watson would not be the next Otto Graham, though. *Joshua Gunter / cleveland.com*

he was booed—on the road and even in Cleveland. There were small anti-Watson demonstrations at various games in that 2022 season. I can't ever recall a player returning to action who received such negative public reaction.

In 2022, Watson looked nothing like the Pro Bowl quarterback he had been in Houston. The Browns talked about him being "rusty," due to the long layoff. But he must also have been feeling hated by fans and media. That was new to him. He had been a favorite son when growing up in Gainesville, Georgia (near Atlanta), and helping Clemson win a national title. In his first four years with Houston, he wasn't criticized about anything.

Watson's public statements after joining the Browns gave the impression he was convinced he had done nothing wrong. He could not understand why Browns fans were reluctant to embrace him as their quarterback. In his mind, he was still the star at Clemson and the star quarterback for Houston. He failed to grasp that many Browns fans thought, *He hasn't done anything for us but bring heartache to this franchise.*

The Browns were shocked at how poorly Watson played. Head coach Kevin Stefanski and general manager Andrew Berry kept insisting Watson worked hard. Stefanski sometimes called Watson "a gym rat," meaning he spent a lot of time at the practice facility working out and studying videos on opposing teams.

In 2023, Watson had some good moments. The Browns had a 4-1 record when Watson played a full game. His best Cleveland game was a 33-31 win in Baltimore. The Browns trailed 17-9 at halftime. Watson had completed only 6 of 20 passes. In the second half, Watson completed all 14 of his passes. He brought the Browns back from a 14-point deficit in the fourth quarter to win the game. This was the Deshaun Watson the Browns dreamed of when they made the huge controversial trade.

"He's a warrior," Stefanski said after the game. "He makes plays when they're not there. Makes unbelievable throws. Never a doubt in his mind how this game was going to turn out."

Never had Stefanski gushed about Watson like that before. Turns out, he never would again.

Three days after that Baltimore game, the Browns announced Watson was done for the season. He needed major shoulder surgery, which was performed Nov. 21, 2023.

In his 2023 post-season press conference, Berry said: "When we made the trade [for Watson], we really looked at it as, 'Hey, this is something that we'll evaluate in like a 10-year time horizon because these guys [quarterbacks] play [a long time].' Obviously, we want him on the field more often than he's been. He can't help the shoulder injuries this year, but we're really pleased with him. He's very talented. He's very hard-working. He's adaptable and we really feel good about him moving forward."

That statement gives clues to how the Browns viewed Watson. He would be their quarterback for a decade. They would be a consistent playoff team and a Super Bowl contender.

That clearly was wildly optimistic thinking. Yes, Watson had a brilliant game (actually a great half) versus Baltimore, but there was very little consistency in 2022 or 2023. But the Browns were stuck with him and decided to stay positive. They believed they had no other choice.

Following the shoulder surgery, Watson returned for the 2024 season. He had a 1-6 record in seven starts. The Browns had the NFL's fourth lowest scoring offense with him at quarterback. He looked shaky, often bolting from the pocket early. His arm lacked strength. He threw only five touchdown passes in his seven starts. His 2024 season ended when he suffered an Achilles injury Oct. 20.

The Browns finished the season with a 3-14 record.

Watson had his first Achilles surgery Oct. 25, 2024. He re-injured his Achilles and had a second surgery Jan. 9, 2025. That led to the Browns writing him out of their plans for the 2025 season.

* * *

At the NFL annual meetings in 2025, Browns owner Jimmy Haslam met with a few Cleveland area reporters. He opened the press conference with these comments:

> Let's address the elephant in the room. We took a big swing and miss with Deshaun. We thought we had the quarterback. We didn't and we gave up a lot of draft picks to get him. So we've got to dig ourselves out of that hole.

Deshaun Watson settled more civil lawsuits (24) than he started games for the Browns (19) between 2022 and 2024. *Joshua Gunter / cleveland.com*

Haslam didn't want to talk about who should be blamed for the Watson move:

> I've said this I think numerous times, Deshaun Watson was an entire organization's decision. It ends with Dee [Haslam] and I, so hold us accountable.

Here's what I heard about the "five-month odyssey," as Berry called the pursuit of Watson. The general manager was enamored by Watson's athletic ability and pass accuracy. When Watson was traded to Cleveland, he had completed 68% of his passes. That was the highest completion percentage in NFL history for any quarterback in the first four years of his career.

Watson originally didn't want to come to Cleveland. After meeting with several teams, his camp publicly eliminated the Browns from consideration. Haslam then greenlighted Berry to call back with the $230 million fully guaranteed offer. No general manager can make a decision of that magnitude on his own.

Of course, the Browns football people could have said, "Maybe we shouldn't go that far—all the draft picks and the money . . ." Perhaps they did. I can't get a clear answer on that. But in the end, it ultimately was an ownership decision because of the money, the negative publicity and draft picks involved in the deal.

At the press conference, Dee and Jimmy Haslam were trying to explain the deal and how it went wrong.

"The player got hurt and so that was an unusual situation," Dee Haslam said. "There were a lot of unusual situations. But really bad injuries when a player has these kind of bad injuries . . . It's really unfortunate for him and unfortunate for our organization."

Yes, injuries were a big part of what happened to Watson.

"He's had three horrific injuries in what, a 15-month period, right?" Jimmy Haslam said. "Shoulder. . . tears his Achilles and re-tears his Achilles. I think the focus now is on getting him healthy and how long does that take and when can he be healthy? So that's the main thing we'd be focused on."

Did sitting out nearly two years (700 days between regular season games) play a role in the injuries? Hard to know.

But this much is certain: Watson hung over the franchise like one huge gloomy cloud. Even after the lawsuits were resolved, the Browns were bombarded with questions about Watson's problems producing on the field.

In 2023, the Browns had an 11-6 record. They won games with four different starting quarterbacks. Watson made six starts. That was the season when Joe Flacco joined the team in November after being out of football since the end of the 2022 season. He started five games. The Browns were 4-1.

In Flacco's five starts, he threw 13 touchdown passes and averaged 323 yards passing per game. He also threw eight interceptions. He thrived in Stefanski's play-action offense. In his six starts, Watson threw seven touchdown passes and averaged 186 yards passing. The contrast was startling, and it reflected poorly on Watson.

As the 2024 season arrived, the Browns decided to junk the Stefanski-style offense that was 12th in the NFL in scoring with those four different quarterbacks winning games. They hired Ken Dorsey to bring in a more wide-open offense, much like Watson had in Houston. Veteran offensive coordinator Alex Van Pelt and other assistant coaches were fired as the Browns searched for a new way to revive Watson. The changes backfired. Good people lost their jobs, and the Browns ended up with the NFL's worst offense in 2024, averaging 15.2 points per game.

The Watson trade was framed as perhaps the worst in NFL history by many media members, not just me. And that is the bottom line on the biggest swing and miss in Browns history.

AL LERNER—GONE TOO SOON

The first time I had a personal conversation with Al Lerner was right after a 1998 press conference. It was held a week after the official announcement that Lerner would be the owner of the new Cleveland Browns expansion team.

"So this is how it's going to be?" Lerner asked me.

To Lerner's credit, he pulled me away from the crowd of other media people. It was, as he'd say, "Man-to-man."

"How's what going to be?" I asked.

"Just tell me now," he said. "Are you going to rip me all the time or what?"

Lerner was staring hard at me, his face red, his voice harsh. The former Marine was channeling his old Parris Island boot camp days.

I had been very critical of Lerner's bid to become the new owner of the Browns. The reason was because Lerner helped Art Modell move the old Browns to Baltimore. That deal was even signed on Lerner's private jet on the runway of the Baltimore-Washington airport. Modell and Baltimore city officials were present on Lerner's plane.

"Al, it's over," I said. "You've got the team. I've had my say. I'm done."

"I don't understand your problem," said Lener.

"I don't understand why you helped Art move to Baltimore," I said. "Both of you have a life here, real roots. I don't get it."

"I was helping a friend," said Lerner.

"There had to be a better way," I said.

"Art had money trouble," said Lerner. "He needed a new stadium. He wanted to keep the team for his family. Baltimore was a way to do it."

"Why not just buy the team?" I asked. "Make him President Emeritus or something."

"He wouldn't sell it to anyone," said Lerner. "He was going to keep it."

The discussion continued for quite a while. Lerner went from being angry to trying to explain his actions. It came down to "trying to help a friend."

Then we hit another sore spot. I had written something about Lerner's quest to buy the new Browns as a way "to get his honor back" after helping Modell take the franchise out of town.

That phrase bothered Lerner, the former Marine. He was out of the school of "once a Marine, always a Marine." Honor ranked with God, country and family among the highest values.

* * *

Al Lerner was more than a former Marine pilot and lieutenant. He was the son of Jewish-Russian immigrants who came to America with no money before World War II. He was the boy who worked in the family sandwich shop/candy store in Brooklyn, New York. The business was closed only three days a year—the high Jewish holidays. The place had six stools and two public phones. Lerner's family never owned their own phone, they used the ones in their little restaurant.

Lerner graduated from Columbia in 1955 and then spent two years in the Marines (1955–57). Lerner returned to New York. He became a furniture salesman for Broyhill, and he was good at it. He moved from New York to Baltimore and finally to Cleveland. He made money. He bought real estate. His first purchase was a Cleveland apartment building.

In 1981, he bought into Equitable bank. He was 48 years old when he moved into the world of finance and investments. He later bought into Maryland National Bank. Using $100 million of his own money, he took what became MBNA public on the stock market. The Associated Press said the initial sales of shares raised $995 million. At the time, MBNA was "the world's largest credit card issuer," according to the Associated Press.

Along the way, he made friends with Art Modell in the 1970s. They began watching Browns games together in Modell's private box at the old Cleveland Stadium. In 1986, Lerner bought 5% of the Browns to help Modell, who already was in financial trouble.

The obvious answer to the Browns' ownership problems in the early 1990s was for Lerner to become the majority owner of the franchise. Modell could not navigate the Cleveland political scene and convince the Powers That Be to build him a new stadium. Lerner was different. He was a forceful man and incredibly rich by this point. He had "juice" with both the business and the Cleveland political machine. He knew how to get things done and understood leverage and power. I believe Lerner as majority owner would have kept the old Browns here . . . in a new stadium.

But that didn't happen. Nor did Lerner tell Modell: "I'm not helping you move the Browns. No way I'm being part of taking the team from the community."

It was Lerner who had connections with the Maryland and Baltimore political communities. He was entrenched in the state's financial system with his ownership of MBNA. Lerner facilitated the Browns' move to Baltimore after the 1995 NFL season.

In 1998, Lerner was worth $2.5 billion . . . huge money . . . when he jumped into the bidding for the new expansion franchise for

Cleveland. The NFL liked Lerner as the new Browns owner. Many league officials came to know him because of his association with Modell. The NFL paired him with former San Francisco 49ers executive Carmen Policy. A Youngstown native, Policy was a wise political operator when it came to dealing with the NFL owners.

At one point, Lerner objected to the NFL owners trying to drive up the price of the franchise. Policy told me that Lerner was ready to back out. Policy convinced him to stay in the bidding.

"Al, this is like when a Rembrandt comes on the market," Policy said he told Lerner. "They're not making any more of them. Once you're in, you're in. The value of the franchise will increase. You'll get caught up in it. The idea that you can do without it after you taste it—that's just not acceptable."

Policy knew Lerner's competitive (and combative) personality would keep him in the bidding game. Lerner was infuriated that Modell was lobbying NFL owners in favor of a group headed by Charles Dolan, who owned the New York Knicks and other holdings. Tribe owner Larry Dolan and his son Paul Dolan also were part of the group.

Lerner could not believe the owner fighting hardest against him was Art Modell. Where was the loyalty? Of course, Browns fans could ask the same question of Lerner . . . where was the loyalty to your adopted hometown when you set up Modell's exit to Baltimore?

Modell was angry that most of the criticism for the move was aimed at him, not Lerner. "Didn't Al advise me to move to Baltimore?" Modell told people.

Lerner was enraged that Modell had turned on him. Lerner had taken some heat in Cleveland for his role with the Browns' move. Where was Modell now, when Lerner could use his support in the ownership bid?

Lerner felt betrayed. By 1998, the men no longer spoke to each other.

Policy told me how Lerner "several times" had helped Modell financially during Modell's days owning the Browns. When the team moved to Baltimore, Modell had to pay $32 million to Lerner—the share of the team Lerner owned.

On Sept. 8, 1998, the NFL had an owners meeting. On the advice of Policy, Lerner offered $530 million for the Browns. A group headed by Charles Dolan offered $500 million.

The first ownership vote was 21 for Lerner, seven for Dolan and two owners abstaining. Modell did not have a vote. But that wasn't enough as 23 were needed to pick a new owner.

Modell finally spoke to the NFL owners as a group and some individually, asking them to support Lerner. The next vote was 29-0 with Oakland's Al Davis abstaining. In the end, Modell did pay back Lerner by helping him secure the needed votes.

The $530 million was the most ever paid for any American pro sports franchise. The previous high had been $311 million for the Los Angeles Dodgers in Major League Baseball.

The Browns were back, now owned by one of the richest men in the country.

* * *

I wrote a book called *False Start* about how the new Browns were set up to fail. Their first game would be Sept. 12, 1999—only 369 days after the sale was announced. The previous two expansion teams—Carolina and Jacksonville—had had more than 600 days to prepare for their first game.

In NFL history, only Dallas (240 days in 1960) and New Orleans (320 days in 1966) had less time to prepare for a season as an expansion team.

"I asked the NFL to postpone it a year," Policy told me. "Move it back to 2000. But the NFL said they promised Cleveland a team by 1999. They had drawn up a schedule with 31 teams [Cleveland being the 31st] and they were not going to change it."

Carmen Policy (left) convinced Al Lerner (right) to stay in the bidding for the new Browns franchise. Unfortunately, he couldn't convince the NFL to give the team more time to build a roster. *Dale Omori / The Plain Dealer*

A lot went wrong in those early days when the Browns were throwing together an NFL team. Policy was trying to hire a big-name general manager and an experienced head coach. Not many of those were available. None were interested in the challenge in Cleveland, even with Lerner willing to pay them lavishly. Policy told me some executives wanted a piece of the ownership, something Lerner refused to relinquish—especially after the ordeal he endured to secure the franchise.

The Browns ended up with Dwight Clark as the GM. He had worked with Policy with the San Francisco 49ers. He had been a mediocre GM at best. That track record continued in Cleveland. Policy was shopping for a veteran head coach. He wanted Steve Mariucci, who was the coach of San Francisco and had three years left on his contract. While Policy said he was open to hiring "the best people," he seemed focused on those he knew from his 49ers days.

Policy studied some coaches from the offensive side of the ball as a possible head coach. His list included Bill Callahan (Oakland),

Brian Billick (Minnesota), Andy Reid (Green Bay), Sherman Lewis (Green Bay) and Chris Palmer (Jacksonville).

From that list, Reid would be hired by Joe Banner (later a Browns CEO) to be the head coach in Philadelphia. Reid would later move on to Kansas City, and his last football stop will eventually be the Hall of Fame in Canton. Callahan became a legendary offensive line coach. He passed through Cleveland (2020–23). Billick turned down the Browns and later won a Super Bowl in Baltimore.

The Browns ended up with Palmer. Like the first draft pick of the new Browns franchise (Tim Couch), Palmer never had a chance.

I quickly became friends with Palmer.

A few days after he became the head coach, I met him at the team's training facility in Berea. He was hired Jan. 21, 1999. The Browns were set to open the season Sept. 12, 1999. That was not even eight full months away.

I went into Palmer's office. He had NFL media guides spread out. He had a yellow legal pad on his desk. He was looking through the media guides, seeking assistant coaches who had recently been fired. He was writing down names. He also was checking the media guide information on coaches who had recently called to apply for a job.

"I have no assistants," he said. "I don't even have a secretary yet."

This was before the internet and cellphones were common. He took me down to what once had been the Browns' weight room. A single barbell was on the floor. The rest of the room was empty.

"They took the weights and everything to Baltimore," said Palmer. "We're supposed to play a game in eight months."

He sighed, then went to work.

At the time Palmer was hired, Palmer knew he was not close to the top of Policy's coaching list. I counted at least five other coaches ranked above him. They turned down the job.

"You know what I heard from most coaches?" Policy asked me. "They wanted to be the second Browns coach."

Palmer expressed the same sentiment to me: "I want to be the guy who replaces me in this job."

That's because they knew the first coach facing the unreasonable timetable to open the season was destined to fail.

Palmer took the job because he was 49. He knew it might be his only chance to be a head coach in the NFL. He didn't play in the league. His coaching career included college stops such as Lehigh, UConn, New Haven and Colgate. His only head coaching experience was at Boston University.

He eventually went into the NFL as an assistant for nine seasons. He moved from the Houston Oilers to the New England Patriots to Jacksonville, where he finally became an offensive coordinator.

I have seen a lot of messed up situations for coaches/managers covering Cleveland sports for more than 50 years. Never were any of them as daunting as what Palmer faced.

Palmer coached for two seasons with records of 2-14 and 3-13.

"After my second season, they [the front office] called me in and wanted to know how many games I thought we'd win the next year," said Palmer. "I said, 'About six.' That's not what they wanted to hear."

I believe the Browns already had targeted another coach before that meeting with Palmer. They wanted Butch Davis, a former Dallas Cowboys defensive coordinator who had spent the previous six years as the head coach of the University of Miami Hurricanes. While Palmer had a 3-13 record with the Browns, Davis led Miami to an 11-1 mark and a No. 2 national ranking in college football polls.

Davis was a disciple of Jimmy Johnson, who had won Super Bowls with the Dallas Cowboys. He was a charismatic figure, a guy who challenged his players to "lay your guts out all over the field."

Davis came in with a lot of power. Clark soon left as general manager. Davis took on the Bill Belichick/Bill Parcells role serving as head coach and de facto GM, even if someone else had the title.

In his first two years, Davis led the Browns to records of 7-9 and 9-7. In 2002, they made the playoffs. That's great progress for an expansion team.

* * *

Few people knew that Lerner was suffering with cancer. In May 2001, he had a brain tumor removed. The initial outlook was supposed to be positive. But it's always hard to know if that was true, or just something for public consumption.

Lerner was in and out of the hospital for the last 15 months of his life. He died Oct. 23, 2002, at the age of 69. He didn't live to see the Browns make the playoffs.

At the time of his death, Lerner's wealth was estimated at $4.3 billion, making him the 36th richest person in America, according to Forbes magazine.

Part of the deal that brought Carmen Policy to Cleveland was Lerner giving him 10% ownership in the franchise. In many ways, Policy acted like the owner. Lerner had complete trust in him.

A 2002 ESPN story by Len Pasquarelli told how Lerner knew he was dying and had prepared his son Randy to take over the franchise.

"There will be no sale of the franchise," wrote Pasquarelli. "The Lerner family will not be strapped by excessive estate taxes . . . the franchise will be under the Lerner family stewardship, clearly for the long term."

In the same ESPN story, Policy was in his best public relations form. He talked about how the Lerner family planned "to own this team for a long time. I would say indefinitely. I would say chances are good you will see the Lerner grandchildren working for this team down the road."

Son Randy Lerner would take over as the owner. He was 40 years old.

"Early word on Randy Lerner is that he's much like his father, who was one of the quietest, most influential of owners" wrote Pasquarelli.

Policy told Pasquarelli that Randy "grew up wearing Cleveland Browns pajamas . . . whose room was a shrine to the Browns."

The fact was, Randy was almost nothing like his father. I realized that when I secured my first one-on-one interview. We met in his office at the Browns' training complex. He had several pieces of modern art on the wall.

Randy Lerner didn't grow up serving ice cream and sandwiches at a little diner. He didn't grow up working 12 hours a day in the family business. He didn't grow up using a pay phone as the family phone. He didn't grow up fighting for every dime, sweating out every business deal until the finances were stable.

The Lerner family lived in Shaker Heights, but not in opulence. For a while, they were in an apartment on Van Aken Boulevard. Randy went to Shaker Heights High. He had part-time jobs in the summer. He went to Browns games as a kid.

His first stop after high school was Clare College in Cambridge. Then he went to Columbia in New York and then graduated with a law degree from Columbia. He is a smart guy, as his academic credentials demonstrate.

When his father owned the team—and later during his 10 years in charge—Randy loved to hug friends, players and coaches after the Browns won. He did take losses hard. He was a true fan. He also had an interest in art. He became a passionate English soccer fan and eventually bought the Aston Villa franchise in 2006.

I had several private conversations with Randy over the years.

Pasquarelli's ESPN story insisted "the apple didn't fall far from the tree" when Randy took over for his father. That was wishful thinking. Al Lerner was focused. Al Lerner understood how to operate in the boardrooms and backrooms. When necessary, he could be a business brawler. He was not afraid to deliver bad news. His leadership style was pure Marine. Randy comes across as a gentle soul who doesn't like conflict. He also likes to jump from topic to topic in conversations, something that frustrated the football people working under him.

Randy Lerner was not at all like his father. Nor was he suited to run a high-pressurized NFL franchise in his hometown. He was sensitive to criticism. He struggled in the few press conferences when he did speak. A lack of public confidence was evident.

He desperately needed Policy's steady hand and guidance, but it became clear Policy wasn't interested in working for Randy.

In 2017, I interviewed Butch Davis about his time in Cleveland.

"Mr. Lerner was spectacular," said Davis. "A great businessman. He was a former Marine. That man was tough. Carmen Policy had been a part of Super Bowl winners in San Francisco."

Davis said Lerner told him that this "was a 10-year job." He was taking over an expansion team that was two years old.

"Listening to Mr. Lerner, I said, 'OK, this is a guy who gets it,' " said Davis.

Lerner died as the Browns were moving toward the 2002 playoffs.

"That changed everything," said Davis. "I don't know all the details, but there were some conflicts between Randy and Carmen Policy. That led to Carmen starting his exit out of there."

As Randy took over, Policy was taking a lesser role with the Browns. Policy had signed a five-year contract to work with Lerner in 1998. Policy helped Lerner hire John Collins to run the business end of the franchise.

On May 1, 2004, Policy announced he was leaving the Browns.

In an April 16, 2015, interview with Crain's Cleveland Business, Policy said: "Once Al died, it was like the air went out of the building in Berea. Everything changed. I was almost at the end of my rope anyway."

* * *

After his father's death, Randy Lerner took over ownership of the Browns. At times he seemed distracted by his English soccer team. Here, he talks with legendary Browns running back Jim Brown during training camp in 2006.
John Kuntz / The Plain Dealer

Lerner kept looking for someone to run the franchise.

After Policy left, Randy gave Butch Davis full power on the football side. That lasted less than two full seasons. Davis quit after a 3-8 start to the 2004 season, blaming "panic attacks." I'm sure he had anxiety. But like Policy, he knew the Browns were in big trouble after the death of Al Lerner.

Randy kept looking for what he often called "a strong leader." He went from Davis to GM Phil Savage (2005–08). He fired Savage before the last game of the 2008 season. Savage was at the Charlotte airport, awaiting a flight to Pittsburgh where the Browns would finish their season. He was talking on the phone to Randy when the owner delivered the news.

In an interview for my book *Browns Blues,* Savage gave me the account of how he decided to go to the game in Pittsburgh anyway. He wanted to meet with Randy in person, trying to change the owner's mind. A few days before being fired, he gave Randy an

Jimmy Haslam III is announced as proud new majority owner of the Browns at a press conference in 2012. *Joshua Gunter / cleveland.com*

update on the search for a new coach. The Browns planned to fire Romeo Crennel after the season. Instead, the Browns fired both.

A few days later, Randy had a press conference telling us about how he needed to find a coach and GM. In the middle of the press conference, word came out that the Jets had fired head coach Eric Mangini. Randy had been spending a lot of time in the New York area. He had a home in the Hamptons. He became excited when learning Mangini was available. Soon, he hired Mangini to coach the Browns and gave him complete power over the roster.

That lasted two years.

Next, Randy brought in Mike Holmgren as team president to be in charge of the entire operation. Holmgren had been a Super Bowl winning coach in Green Bay. Holmgren told me that Randy sometimes wanted him to "act as owner." That role was no longer attractive to Randy, whose English soccer team also had big problems.

Randy bought the soccer franchise in 2006 when the franchise was in the Premier League. He sold it in 2016 when it was relegated to a lower division.

Forbes magazine reported: “The former owner of the NFL’s Cleveland Browns is selling his English soccer team, Aston Villa, for $90 million. Since buying the team in 2006 for $125 million, Lerner has pumped close to $300 million into the team and Aston Villa has cost him $100,000 a day to run.”

Forbes estimated his loss on the deal was $400 million.

I kept hearing that Randy promised his family he’d keep the Browns for 10 years. He did just that. Al Lerner died Oct. 23, 2002. Randy sold the team to Jimmy Haslam Oct. 16, 2012.

The sale was an interesting financial deal. The price was announced as $1 billion. But Haslam paid only $600 million upfront. The remaining $400 million was due four years later. Joe Banner served the same role for Haslam as Policy had for Al Lerner. He worked with the NFL and helped Haslam secure the franchise. He also had a strong say in the structure of the deal, which gave Haslam four years of the NFL’s lucrative TV income before he had to pay the final $400 million.

In the 10 years Randy Lerner owned the Browns, the team had a 53-105 record and one winning season (10-6 in 2007).

In 2025, Forbes magazine estimated Randy Lerner’s net worth at $1.2 billion.

WRONG TIME, WRONG TEAM: TIM COUCH

The 1999 Sports Illustrated NFL draft preview edition featured a photo of Akili Smith, Tim Couch and Browns superfan Big Dawg holding a huge bone.

The big headline on the cover was: "A Bone to Pick."

"Only days before they were to make the No. 1 pick in the NFL draft, the reborn Browns were torn between passers Tim Couch and Akili Smith."

The story was by Peter King, a sensational NFL writer for decades with various publications.

For younger fans, it's hard to remember the excitement about the Browns returning as an expansion team and being awarded the first pick in the 1999 NFL draft. It came four years after the sports trauma of the original Cleveland Browns moving to Baltimore.

The Browns returned because an amazing thing happened: Northeast Ohio politicians of both parties, people of every racial and economic status and many in the national media came together to scream: BROWNS FANS WERE SCREWED! GIVE CLEVELAND ANOTHER NFL TEAM!

And the NFL did just that, handing the Browns an expansion franchise for the 1999 season. They even allowed the Browns to keep their original name. Former Browns owner Art Modell took credit for that, but I disagree. While writing about the Browns' move for my book *False Start,* I found a Baltimore Sun story with a headline including the words "Baltimore Browns."

Baltimore ended up becoming the Ravens.

The new Browns began searching for a quarterback.

Question: Who started at quarterback for the Browns in their final game in 1995 as the old Cleveland Browns?

Answer: Vinny Testaverde.

Confession: I couldn't remember and had to look it up. The game was played in Jacksonville. The Browns lost, 24-21. Testaverde threw a 39-yard touchdown pass to Michael Jackson. He scored on a quarterback sneak. But he also heaved three interceptions. The Browns finished that season at 5-11.

Three years later, the Browns (at least in name) were back. Team President Carmen Policy, GM Dwight Clark and head coach Chris Palmer were debating who should be the top pick of the new franchise.

They could take anyone in the draft. They had agreed on the choice being a quarterback. A new team . . . a new quarterback who is the top draft pick . . . that sounded like a wise idea. There were several highly rated quarterbacks in that draft. Five would be selected in the top 12.

Who should the Browns select?

Early in the draft process, the Browns eliminated Syracuse quarterback Donovan McNabb. Palmer wasn't impressed with McNabb. Because Palmer had been a successful quarterbacks coach and offensive coordinator, he was given a loud voice in determining whom the Browns would draft.

So McNabb was out.

Along with Couch, other names considered were Akili Smith, Daunte Culpepper and Cade McNown. Soon, the Browns had narrowed the selection process to Couch and Smith.

* * *

Before deciding between Couch and Smith, the Browns received an unprecedented trade offer.

Calling the Browns was Mike Ditka, who was running the New Orleans Saints as head coach and general manager. He was offering his *entire 1999 draft* for the top pick. He planned to take Texas running back Ricky Williams.

The Browns had brought in Williams for a pre-draft visit. But they would have had no intention of drafting him. Policy was hyping the draft, the Browns letting the media know about the various college players being considered by the team . . . even if the interest was marginal.

Policy didn't like the trade offer, even though it made some sense for an expansion team that needed as many draft picks as possible. The Saints were offering picks in the first, third, fourth, fifth, sixth and seventh rounds.

"When you have a chance to draft a franchise quarterback, you do it," said Policy.

Washington took Ditka's offer, and squeezed even more out of the desperate Saints. For the No. 5 pick, Washington received the No. 12 pick along with five other selections in the 1999 draft. And they also convinced the Saints to trade their first and third-round picks in 2000.

Suppose the Browns had made that trade. They would have had the No. 12 overall picks in 1999 and—hard to believe—the No. 2 pick overall in 2000 . . . because New Orleans had a terrible 1999 season. With the No. 12 pick, they could have selected Antoine Winfield from Ohio State (and Akron Garfield High School). The defensive back made three Pro Bowl teams and played 13 seasons. They also would have had a pair of third-round picks, along with selections in the fourth, fifth, sixth and seventh rounds. That's not all—they would have had the rest of their own draft picks, too!

Modern analytics would have loved that trade. Of course, you

Talented, but doomed from the start. "The fans have more an appreciation for me now than when I played there," Tim Couch says today.
David I. Andersen / The Plain Dealer

still have to pick the right players for it to work out. Nonetheless, the more picks a team has, the more likely a team would find some talent in what would be the Mr. Big Volume approach. You probably would get lucky a few times. But the Browns were in a unique position as an expansion franchise in a city that had lost its team three years earlier. It's hard to remember the emotional condition of many Browns fans in 1999. They were bitter at former Browns owner Art Modell for moving the team. They were angry at the NFL for allowing the franchise to move to Baltimore.

"The Move" haunted the franchise.

Policy wanted to sell hope and sizzle. Having the first overall pick with a brand-new franchise did just that. Trading down to No. 12 and adding all those other picks . . . that would have been wise for an expansion team, but what about the fan base needing someone to believe in?

Policy wanted that "someone" to be a quarterback . . . the first pick in the draft . . . the fresh face of the new franchise.

Early in the process, Policy favored Couch. He'd watched Couch play in his home state of Kentucky, leading the 1998 University of Kentucky Wildcats football team to its first winning season in eight years. Kentucky played in its first New Year's bowl game in 46 years. Couch had been in the public eye dating back to his high school days at Kentucky's Leslie County High. He was the Kentucky Mr. Football high school player of the year in football. In basketball, he averaged 36 points a game on the court as a sweet-shooting 6-foot-5 forward. The Kentucky basketball team said he could also play for them if he went to Kentucky to play quarterback. If Couch wanted to skip football, Kentucky basketball coach Rick Pitino said he'd give Couch a basketball scholarship.

Nearly every major college football program wanted Couch. He stayed home in Kentucky to revive the football team in his home state.

But there were concerns. In the Sports Illustrated story, Peter King wrote:

> After throwing for 8,159 yards and 73 touchdowns in his last two Kentucky seasons, Couch has been painted as this year's Peyton Manning—polished on and off the field . . . But because Couch directed a variation of the run-and-shoot at Kentucky, it's difficult to predict how suited his game is to the NFL. At least half of his collegiate passes were dump-offs, screens, curls or short crossing routes; last season 74% of his 553 attempts traveled 10 yards downfield or less. Andre Ware and David Klingler, the seventh and sixth picks out of Houston in 1990 and 1992, respectively, were run-and-shoot quarterbacks who flopped (after playing in that style of college offense) in the NFL.

* * *

Akili Smith.

Many Browns fans don't know the name . . . or it's a vague memory.

When it came time for the Browns to make the top pick in the draft, they nearly took a guy who has been one of the draft's biggest busts . . . ever.

No one knew that coming into the 1999 draft, of course. The Browns were very intrigued with Smith.

"Smith played in an orthodox NFL-style offense in college (Oregon), and he blew away the competition in 1998 with a 32-touchdown passes, eight-interception season," King wrote in his Sports Illustrated draft preview. "Last year, Smith averaged an NCAA-high 10.1 yards per attempt, Couch a pedestrian 7.1. [Browns Coach] Chris Palmer, the former offensive coordinator for the Jacksonville Jaguars, will use a multiple offense that will rely more on intermediate and deep throws than most NFL teams use, maybe making Smith a better fit for the Browns."

That report was accurate. I recall Palmer telling me how drafting Couch would require the Kentucky product to make a major adjustment from college.

Why not take Smith?

The Browns looked at his background. He was a Parade Magazine All-American as a high school player in San Diego. He didn't have the standardized test scores to attend a four-year college. He was such a gifted athlete, he was drafted at the age of 17 in the seventh round in 1993 by the Pittsburgh Pirates to play baseball. Smith spent three years in the minors. He could never progress above rookie ball, hitting .176 (.521 OPS) in 225 pro plate appearances.

Baseball was over. Smith enrolled at Grossmont Junior College to play quarterback for two years. He was a star and was heavily recruited. He signed with Oregon and worked to raise his grades and became eligible to play. He was a part-time starter as a junior, then had off-field problems before his senior season.

"Smith was suspended from the football program for two months before the 1998 season after being arrested for driving under the influence and getting into a bar fight—separate incidents within a week of each other," King wrote. "(He was acquitted of all charges in the bar fight, and the DUI charges were dropped when he agreed to enter an alcohol diversion program.)"

With the Ducks, Smith played in 21 games. He became a full-time starter as a senior. His rise was quick and epic when it came to NFL draft boards.

"Until he burst onto the scene last season, when he threw for 3,763 yards and led 8-3 Oregon to the Aloha Bowl, Smith lived in relative obscurity," King wrote. "While jogging with a teammate one day last September, he spoke with envy about quarterbacks Cade McNown of UCLA and Brock Huard of Washington being on the cover of a preseason football magazine. 'I hope I get a free-agent shot after school, or maybe get picked in the sixth or seventh round,' Smith recalls saying."

The Browns correctly worried about Smith being able to handle the pressure and public spotlight of being the top pick in the draft and playing in football-obsessed Cleveland for an expansion team. Couch, having lived in the public eye since early in his high school days, was more equipped for that.

* * *

Couch also wanted to be the first pick. He told his agent (Cleveland-based Tom Condon) to make the deal. This was before the rookie salary cap, something worth repeating because it's a key part of this story. In the 1990s, top draft picks walked into their new teams already making more money than 80% or more of their new teammates. That sometimes was the product of a holdout, which created animosity from veterans.

"You are just elated with a chance to be picked first," Couch told me. "It's a surreal moment. You never think growing up about being the No. 1 pick in the draft. You're thrilled and kind of worried at the same time."

The Browns told the agents for Smith and Couch that their clients would have to sign before the draft. The Browns had Couch as their top pick and first went to him to cut a deal. He agreed to a seven-year, $48 million deal. All that was guaranteed was the $12.25 million signing bonus. That doesn't sound like much, but the average NFL player was paid about $1 million in 1999.

After Couch was selected, I wrote:

> Tim Couch is signed, sealed and delivered. This is how an NFL team does business. You have the No. 1 pick. You don't take any chances with a long holdout, angry agents and jealous players. If you're Browns owner Al Lerner, you set the agenda. You tell Tim Couch, "You can play in a football mad-city in front of sellout crowds or you can go to the town where quarterbacks die—Cincinnati."
>
> You tell the No. 1 pick that you're giving him a healthy 8% raise over last year's top pick . . .

In the same story I dwelled on how well the new Browns had handled the draft right from the business perspective.

I recalled the last time the Browns had been in the draft. That was in 1995. They traded popular running back Eric Metcalf to Atlanta for the No. 10 pick. They wanted Penn State tight end Kyle Brady. When Brady was picked at No. 9, Bill Belichick (running the Browns draft) was so angry, he traded the No. 10 pick to San Francisco for the No. 30 pick. He insisted there wasn't a big difference between the No. 10 and No. 30 pick. To be fair, the Browns did also receive San Francisco's top pick in the 1996 draft as part of that deal. When it came time to make that selection, though, the franchise was in Baltimore. Meanwhile, Belichick made Ohio State linebacker Craig Powell the Browns' 1995 selection at No. 30. At one point in Powell's rookie season, Belichick proclaimed, "Powell seems to be lost in the weeds." Powell played a grand total of 14 NFL games spread over three seasons.

* * *

Most Browns fans know the story of Couch—he was doomed to fail. Being a starting rookie quarterback on an expansion team is nothing any player can imagine. Couch was being compared to Peyton Manning. "Almost Brett Favre-like playmaking ability," is how he was described in an April 4, 1999, USA Today story.

On draft night, Browns GM Dwight Clark said: "Tim Couch has always been the guy. He has always been the leader. He's been the guy who rallied the troops. He was the best basketball player on his team. He set records in high school. He set records in college. We expect him to set records here."

It's impossible to recreate the frenzy from the fans and media over that first draft for the new Browns.

I covered the entire 1999 draft, including the Browns' 11 selections. Guess how many were offensive linemen?

Zero.

I never wrote about that back then. I probably didn't notice it—until the team began playing games. Yes, they added some veterans in free agency and the expansion draft, but not picking a single offensive lineman in the college draft was a major error.

"It takes a while before reality sets in," Couch told me. "When it does, you realize, 'Man, I'm on the worst team in the league!' "

The plan in Couch's rookie season was for veteran quarterback Ty Detmer to start for several games as Couch became accustomed to the NFL. At least that was the idea of the front office.

The Browns opened the season with Pittsburgh at the new Browns Stadium. Thanks a lot, NFL. The league could not have come up with a worse home opener for the expansion franchise. The Browns were behind 20-0 at the half. In the fourth quarter, Couch replaced Detmer.

The Browns lost 43-0. They had 9 yards rushing. They had 52 yards passing. They had *two* first downs. Couch threw three passes, two incomplete and one an interception.

Palmer told me that he decided to play Couch because the team was awful. "Let's get him some experience and something good out of the season. The best way for a quarterback to grow is to play."

The Browns were 2-12 in the games started by Couch. He was sacked 56 times, the most in the NFL in 1999.

"Once the season got going, I felt the pressure of being the No. 1 pick," Couch said. "With every performance, you feel like you have to prove why you were selected over everyone else in the draft . . . like you have to be perfect. That's a terrible way to think. I got over that by my second year, but . . . "

Couch paused and thought about his time with the Browns.

"I'd never dealt with failure before the Browns," he said. "Coming out of high school, I was the No. 1 [college] recruit in the country. In college, I was the SEC Player of the Year and a finalist for the Heisman Trophy. Then I got to the pros, we were losing games and I wasn't putting up numbers . . . I felt like I was letting people down."

* * *

It's easy to write off Couch's career in Cleveland. Very few fans and media people realized that in 2001 and 2002 (his third and fourth seasons), the Browns had a 15-15 record when he started.

"I was a young player thrown into a new team where I was the starter in the second game of the season," Couch said. "I had some good games, but couldn't sustain it. Once I'd start to build something, I got hurt."

I asked Couch to list his major injuries:

Two shoulder surgeries.

A broken thumb.

A broken foot.

A broken leg.

Too many concussions to count.

"We got to the playoffs in my fourth year [2002] and I broke my leg right before the end of the regular season," he said. "I couldn't play in the playoff game . . . that really hurt."

He played his last NFL game in 2003 at the age of 26. Too many injuries ended his career.

Through it all, Couch still loves the Browns. He watches their games. He hears lots of positive things from fans on social media and when he comes to Cleveland.

"The fans have more an appreciation for me now than when I played there," he said. "They realize it wasn't my fault. We were just a young team trying to figure it out."

Couch once told me that he wondered what it would have been like to be in the position of Ben Roethlisberger, the Miami (Ohio) University product who was drafted by Pittsburgh. Roethlisberger went to an established team with a great coaching staff and lots of talented players. Couch said he didn't mean to say he would have the same career as Roethlisberger, who likely will make the Hall of Fame. But he also knows his career would have been different . . . and better.

Couch has a successful business career in Lexington, where he lives. It's also the home of the University of Kentucky. Overall, life has been good to Couch, although he's had several post-football surgeries.

"I was the first in a long list of [Browns] quarterbacks," said Couch. "There were some good players on that list. They were just guys in the wrong place at the wrong time to make it work in Cleveland."

* * *

What about Akili Smith?

The Bengals selected him with the No. 3 pick overall. He held out and missed nearly all of training camp—a bad move by his agent. He signed a seven-year, $56 million contract with $10.8 million guaranteed.

The Bengals were 39-89 in the eight years before Smith arrived.

Smith had a career 3-14 record as a starter over four years for the Bengals. He was sacked 59 times. He threw only five touchdown passes compared to 13 interceptions.

Later in life, Smith coached several high school teams. His son is Akili Smith Jr. Like his father, he's a quarterback. The son was a highly rated high school recruit and enrolled at Oregon (his father's alma mater) in 2025.

FANS WRITE IN ABOUT TIM COUCH . . .

He had the skill set to be successful, but seemed doomed from Day One. No offensive line, no receivers, no running game, yet he was expected to be successful.

— Ron Pruchnicki

Unfortunately, his career was marked by poor rosters and significant injuries, and he has been tagged as one of the biggest draft busts in history. However, Tim Couch is the only quarterback in NFL history to have two Hail Mary passes of over 50 yards with 0:00 on the clock to win games!

— Jeff McConnell, Bowling Green, Ohio

I really liked Tim Couch. He was dumped into the worst possible situation and somehow survived getting the crap kicked out of him for the better part of five years. He would have been a very good NFL quarterback if he had landed in a better situation. Although, to be honest, I thought the Browns should have drafted McNabb or Akili Smith over him at the time. I'm not sure McNabb would have fared any better and, let's face it, Smith couldn't have fared any worse.

— Dwight Jellison, Canton, Ohio

My opinion on Tim Couch changed a lot with the benefit of hindsight. Obviously his results on the field were not great. But, looking back after his career ended, I realized the ridiculous difficulty of his situation. His supporting cast was abysmal and he took a horrific pounding, but he never made excuses and always seemed to give his best effort. I now have nothing but respect for Tim Couch and would have liked to see what he could have done with a decent team around him.

— Bob Heintel, Monroe, North Carolina

His throw in New Orleans—that Hail Mary—was a thing of beauty. He sadly is just one in a long line of QBs that came, saw, and got conquered.

— Lynn Foor, Mentor, Ohio

Right guy, wrong time. He paid for the sins of Art Modell taking the team away and having to start fresh. I'll always wonder if he could have been great with a supporting cast of established guys. The hits he took were brutal and the fans did him wrong when he got hurt. I hope he doesn't hold it against us but I wouldn't blame him if he does.

— Matt Barnes, Tulsa, Oklahoma

THE VOICE OF THE BROWNS: JIM DONOVAN

I miss Jim Donovan.

I bet many of you reading this book feel the same way.

Donovan passed away from leukemia and some other forms of cancer Oct. 26, 2024.

Jim Donovan became the radio voice of the Browns when the franchise returned in 1999. For the next 23 years, he did the games with former Browns tackle Doug Dieken.

In the summer of 2022, I wanted to write something different about the Browns—something upbeat. I thought about the magic of radio, which is special in the NFL. For television, the national networks send in their own broadcasters to do the games. The voices on TV feel like strangers.

Not radio. The Browns pick the broadcasters, and they are Cleveland-based. In the case of Donovan and Dieken, they were also loved by Browns fans. They were our eyes at the game. They reflected our moods, rejoicing in the precious few victories and agonizing over the seemingly endless seasons of losses.

I had written a lot about Dieken over the years, but never Donovan. I knew Donovan was from Boston. I knew he had been at WKYC, TV-3 reporting on sports in Cleveland since 1985. I knew him casually, even did some TV shows as a guest with him.

But I really knew little about Donovan, other than he had been fighting leukemia for a long time.

I called Donovan and asked if I could come to his house. I didn't say what I had in mind, which was a long profile. I knew Donovan would probably turn it down. Like many of us in the media, he was more comfortable telling other people's stories than his own.

I said it would be, "Just a nice little story before Browns training camp opened."

He invited me over. It took a few minutes to get him talking, but Donovan opened up when I said, "I really want to know, how did you get into the broadcasting business?"

* * *

Imagine being at an NBA game. Next to you are a father and his son. The son's seat is on the aisle, the father next to him. The son is holding a microphone and a tape recorder.

Right before the game begins, the son speaks into the microphone, setting the scene. He gives the lineups and key stats, and prepares for the national anthem.

The son is 12 years old.

"That was me as a kid at Boston Garden," said Donovan.

"I first started watching Boston Bruins games on TV with the sound turned off," he said. "I'd do play-by-play into my cassette tape recorder. But I realized I needed fan noise to make the broadcast more authentic. So I asked my dad if I could take the tape recorder to the Bruins games. We had season tickets."

Donovan said they sat in Section 77, Row F, seats 12-13. They were on the aisle in the Boston Garden balcony.

"I went to every game with four D-batteries for the cassette recorder and two 90-minute cassette tapes," he said. "I'd call the game from my seat, then take it home and listen to it all night long. For 11 years, I went to every Bruins home game. I was there the day Bobby Orr scored the winning goal in the Stanley Cup. It was Mother's Day, 1970."

Donovan was remembering when he used to listen to late-night out-of-town games on his transistor radio from his home in Milton, Massachusetts. One of his favorites was Joe Tait doing Cavs games on 50,000-watt WWWE (1100-AM).

"His scoreboard show was mesmerizing," said Donovan. "Joe had all the stats . . . shots taken . . . minutes played . . . rebounds . . . and he rattled them off. I loved it."

As Donovan talked, we sat on the porch of his 12-acre home overlooking a horse barn and pasture in a Cleveland suburb. ("It's the Ponderosa Ranch," said good friend Doug Dieken, who retired after 34 years doing color commentary for Browns games.)

"I'd send those cassette tapes to all these great announcers in Boston," said Donovan. "They all answered. I'd get an envelope with 'WBZ . . . Boston' . . . it was so great. They'd give me advice like, 'You can't call every place the puck goes.' . . . I did that for years."

How about the fans sitting near him?

"They were great," said Donovan. "They'd ask me stuff like, 'Can you replay that goal by Phil Esposito?' My father [Jim Donovan Sr.] worked for the phone company. I never knew how he got those Bruin season tickets.

"Back then, you could get into a Celtics game any time you wanted. Not the Bruins. Those tickets were like slabs of gold. I bet someone, somewhere was getting free phone service thanks to my dad."

* * *

It's easier to become a pro athlete than to become a team's radio play-by-play voice. There are only a few of those jobs in each city.

"If you get one, you keep it," said Donovan. "People don't leave very often, and they can do it for years and years."

Donovan came from a working-class Irish Catholic family. He had part-time jobs such as being a bagger at the Star Market in the Boston neighborhood of Dorchester.

"I played baseball in high school, but I wanted to do games on the radio," he said. "My parents probably thought, 'He'll outgrow this.' But I never did."

And those tapes he made at Boston Garden as a teenager?

"I used them when I went to Boston University to get the hockey job on the student radio station," said Donovan. "Hockey is a big deal at BU. They had great teams."

Donovan also met future shock jock Howard Stern in college.

"Howard was a senior when I was a freshman," said Donovan. "He had a show on the student station after the hockey games. He did a show called the King Schmaltz Bagel Hour. He had me doing Marv Albert imitations. Lots of the students were from New York, and they loved Albert (who did the Knicks and other games)."

Dieken said Donovan reminded him of the late Nev Chandler, the Browns' radio broadcaster from 1985 to 1993.

"Jimmy and Nev never did jokes," said Dieken. "But they did imitations, especially imitations of other broadcasters. It's hilarious."

While in college, Donovan was hired by a small radio station in the Boston suburb of Marlborough to do high school football games.

"It cost me more money in gas to drive there than they paid me," he said.

Donovan graduated with a degree in broadcast journalism. He needed a job.

"I had no doubt I wanted to do radio, but I also knew Boston was a really big market," said Donovan. "I knew I was going to have to hit the road. For a graduation gift, my parents gave me a subscription to a magazine called Broadcasting. In the back were classified ads."

He found a huge one reading: "One of America's Four Great Radio Stations Seeks a Sports Director!"

Where was it?

"WJON in St. Cloud, Minnesota," said Donovan, who needed a map to find it.

"I sent my hockey tapes out there and they called me," said

Browns fans loved the sheer joy Jim Donovan (left) brought to the games. He was the voice of the team for 23 years, along with former Browns tackle Doug Dieken (right). *Chuck Crow / The Plain Dealer*

Donovan. "I went out for the interview, flew home and they called and offered me the job."

This was 1978. The salary was $10,000.

"But we have a deal," said the station manager. "We'll let you drive this car. It's a Fiat with the station call letters on it. We're going to knock the salary down to $8,500."

It was an offer Donovan couldn't refuse . . . because he had no other offers.

"I couldn't even tell my parents what they were paying me," he said. "They would have been furious. I lived in the basement of a family's house. My parents came to visit me, saw where I was living and they were frightened. They kept saying, 'Are you sure you want to do this?' "

In St. Cloud, Donovan often shivered but never wavered in his dream of doing big league play-by-play somewhere. He did the morning sports show and the afternoon sports show. The station carried 100 games a year. High school football. High school basketball. Hockey. American Legion baseball. Some college sports.

"I was out every night doing every sport," he said. "I remember driving through a whiteout blizzard to Brainerd, Minnesota, to do a hockey game. It's a night game. I get there and it's an outdoor rink. I asked, 'Where is the press box?' They said, 'There is none. . . . You do it from the penalty box.'

"I spent two cold years in St. Cloud."

* * *

After St. Cloud, Donovan's next stop was Burlington, Vermont. He did radio and television during his six years on Lake Champlain. He also called Saint Michael's College basketball games and Class AA minor league baseball games for the Burlington Reds (they are now the Akron RubberDucks).

While doing television in Vermont, he was spotted by a young, aggressive agent named Ken Lindner, who worked at the prestigious William Morris Agency. Lindner began finding opportunities for Donovan. One was with WKYC in Cleveland.

"I had never been to Cleveland before," said Donovan. "The day I came in for the interview, they had about a foot of snow. I came from Vermont, where they love snow."

Donovan wasn't sure about Cleveland. The reservations had nothing to do with the city.

"Jim Mueller was the main guy, and Wayland Boot was the other sportscaster," said Donovan. "They offered me the weekend sports job. I wanted to do radio play-by-play, but that wasn't part of the deal."

Donovan considered turning it down and going back to Vermont.

"My father was very involved and he said, 'You can get stuck up there watching the parade go by. You need to take a chance,' " said Donovan.

He took the job in 1985, and it was a life-changing decision.

"TV-3 was owned by NBC," said Donovan. "Back then, a network could only own five stations. They owned New York, Los Angeles, Chicago, Washington and Cleveland. There were a lot of open doors because of that. TV-3 was down in the ratings. The feeling was people came there to pass through and go on to a bigger city. There was a revolving door.

"People said, look at TV-8 and TV-5. The same people are there forever. Viewers get comfortable with them. They make an appointment in their homes to watch the news."

Donovan did the sports and news each weekday for 39 years. He also did some regular news shows.

When Donovan arrived in Cleveland, TV-3 had the preseason rights to two TV Browns games.

"Gib Shanley had left Cleveland to go to L.A. Now he was coming back to Cleveland," said Donovan. "TV-3 let Gib do the play-by-play. [Former Browns receiver] Reggie Rucker would do the color. I was like the host, the third guy in the booth . . . setting up the start of the game."

This was 1985, Bernie Kosar's NFL rookie season—and the quarterback's first preseason game.

"It was in San Diego," said Donovan. "I was supposed to meet Gib at the pool to prepare for the game. I'd gone back and listened to tapes of the Kardiac Kids (1980), and he had incredible calls.

"This guy walks up with a cigarette hanging out of his mouth," recalled Donovan.

"Are you Jim Donovan?" said Shanley.

"Yes."

"I'm Gib Shanley," he said. "Where's the depth chart?"

Donovan pulled it out and they went to work. Donovan was nervous. Shanley was all business. He did use Donovan at times during the broadcast.

A few days later, he received a note from Shanley: "Jim, I really enjoyed working with you. You did a great job. Looking forward to our next game in Buffalo [two weeks later]. I hope things are going well for you in Cleveland. You have a great future ahead of you."

* * *

Want to know how Donovan became so ready to make just the right call during a Browns game?

One day after a Browns practice, Andre Knott was walking to the parking lot. About 30 feet ahead of him was Jim Donovan, the team's radio voice.

"It sounded like Jimmy was talking to himself," said Knott. "Then I heard him say, 'Brandon Marshall catches a pass at the 10, he's up to the 15 . . . to the 20 . . . and tackled by . . .' "

Knott was the Browns' radio sideline reporter from 2004 to 2010. He now has the same job for the Cleveland Guardians telecasts.

"I realized Jimmy was practicing for the game he'd call on Sunday," said Knott. "He worked on pronouncing names right. Jimmy makes it all sound natural, but it's the product of preparation."

Other media members have heard Donovan in the back of the press room, practicing his opening remarks for a report he planned to file. He believes practicing can make reporting seem natural.

"We'd be in a car together and Jimmy would find a game on the radio," Dieken said. "It didn't matter what sport. He'd listen for a while, then imitate the broadcaster. Sometimes, it was funny. He loves listening to anyone talk about any game."

"That's true," said Knott. "But Jimmy also paid attention to what other broadcasters did, looking for things to make him better. I learned so much from being around Jimmy."

At 7 p.m., he anchored the news desk for the "Front Row" show, which ran for 30 minutes. That was after he did the sports news earlier in the broadcast.

"One of the amazing things about Jimmy was he didn't use a

teleprompter," said Jeff Yakawiak, his producer at WKYC since 2005. "He prepared what we're going to do, then talked. I was in his ear telling him how much time he has left, but that was it. This is rare."

Donovan said that's because of his early career doing radio.

"When you do play-by-play, you have to learn how to improvise," he explained.

When Donovan arrived in Cleveland from Burlington in 1985, Nev Chandler was the Browns' radio play-by-play man.

Donovan began doing the weekend sportscasts on Channel 3. It didn't take long for NBC to begin using Donovan on its NFL telecasts as a play-by-play man for regional games.

"My heart was in play-by-play for one team," said Donovan. "I listened to Nev and loved his work. He was fantastic. You could see the game, listening to him. And Nev was great to me on a personal level."

That's not always the case in broadcasting. Chandler was a rival sports broadcaster at WEWS, TV-5. Donovan was a newcomer in town from Boston. Chandler was great to Donovan—as he was to so many broadcasters and journalists starting out in the Cleveland market. (I include myself in that group.)

"Great announcers on radio have a rhythm," said Donovan. "Every game is different and you have to find the rhythm of that game. A tight game, it's easy. But Nev could find the right rhythm for any game. You have to know the names, the numbers, the information . . . but you need a timing aspect."

Donovan was covering the Browns for WKYC during the week, then flying to another NFL venue for the NBC broadcast.

"I got to town during the Bernie Kosar years," he said. "Nev called those games in front of 78,000 screaming fans. I remember thinking, 'Nev is the luckiest guy in the world. He's got it, that's the job. The TV sports and voice of the Browns on radio . . . the dream daily double.'"

But Donovan also knew that play-by-play jobs rarely come open. Chandler kept his until he died of colon cancer in 1994 at the age of 47. Casey Coleman replaced Chandler and called the games until the Browns moved after the 1995 season to Baltimore.

When the Browns returned as an expansion team in 1999, the new front office led by CEO Carmen Policy wanted to start fresh with a new play-by-play voice. Donovan knew he was considered "a TV guy," and that could count against him for the Browns' radio job.

"I called NBC and said I needed radio tapes to show I could do it," said Donovan. "NBC was no longer doing the NFL [in 1999], but they had Notre Dame football. So I went to a studio and did a Notre Dame game as if it were on the radio. That's what I used for the audition to get in the door."

Previously, under former owner Art Modell, the Browns would put a TV guy in the radio booth to call the games. Examples were Jim Mueller, Jim Graner, Gib Shanley, Chandler and Coleman. They all worked at various Cleveland TV stations.

But this was a new ownership.

"Like everybody else . . . and I mean there was everybody else . . . I wanted to get that job," said Donovan. "They had a lot of auditions. They called you into a TV studio. They had a game on tape, and you called it with a different guy."

Donovan said it was a game between the Eagles and Giants for his audition. He did a quarter with former Browns players Hanford Dixon and Bob Golic. He also called a quarter with WTAM radio host Mike Snyder.

"There might have been someone else," said Donovan. "But I never auditioned with Doug (Dieken), and he ended up getting the job with me."

Dieken had been doing color commentary on the Browns since 1985. Dieken and Donovan were paired up with Coleman doing the sideline reporting.

It didn't take long for Donovan to establish himself as the voice of the Browns. Fans loved his enthusiasm, even with the miserable teams of the expansion years. He also blended in well with Dieken and Coleman.

"Casey was good at being a sideline guy," said Donovan. "He was a newshound. He wasn't just saying, 'It's cold,' like some guys do. He was happy to be back doing the Browns even if it wasn't in the role he'd have preferred. It was never brought up. He was unbelievably classy."

Coleman had that job from 1999 to 2005. He died in 2006 of pancreatic cancer at 55.

"I took over for Casey," said Knott. "I learned so much from Jimmy. He got to know about every guy on the roster. He knew you could learn a lot from the linemen, the tight ends—the guys not interviewed that often. I believe God put Jimmy in my life to help me learn how to be a broadcaster—and I never heard Jimmy put down another play-by-play guy."

* * *

Donovan had a huge fan in Tom Hamilton, the voice of the Guardians who is in the media wing of the Baseball Hall of Fame.

Hamilton worked in small Wisconsin radio markets such as Appleton, Shell Lake and Watertown before moving up to Columbus, Ohio, and finally Cleveland in 1990 to do Major League Baseball.

"You can tell he's a radio guy," Hamilton said. "When you come up like that, you learn to do it all. It's why Jimmy was good at so many things. He could have moved up higher at NBC. He did Olympic work at the network level. Lots of guys are either good on TV or good on radio. Very few like Jimmy are good at both."

Donovan's producer Yakawiak explained: "On TV, the pictures tell the story. You are there to fill in the gaps. On radio, you have to paint the picture with your voice. You are the eyes at the event. Jimmy could switch from one medium to the other making it look easy. It's not."

Yakawiak sounds in awe when he told the story of the Cavs' victory parade after they won the 2016 NBA title. They were *on the air for 10 hours!* Donovan served as the anchor the entire time.

Others at Channel 3 have stories of the night an anchor became ill and Donovan was pressed into service doing hours of election coverage. Listening, you'd have thought it was his regular assignment for the night, rather than being forced into the game as an emergency quarterback.

But for Donovan, his heart is with radio play-by-play and the Browns.

"On radio, the play-by-play guy is the guy," said Dieken. "Fans are not there just to hear [the color analyst]. They want to know what's going on in the game. Jimmy painted such a great picture, you just fill in here and there."

Dieken seemed to be joking when he said: "I'll be listening to him, being entertained . . . forget to talk. Then I realized I had better say something."

That happened when Donovan would draw Dieken into the broadcast with a question. Dieken said Donovan knew football, "but didn't act like he knew everything. He was always asking questions."

One of Donovan's most notable calls was "RUN, WILLIAM . . . RUN!" That was in the final game of 2002 when the Browns were battling for a playoff spot.

"It was a cold, gray, windy, snow blustery day," recalled Donovan. "It was a big game. It felt like the Kosar years in the late 1980s. Then William [Green] busted that run . . . and I was yelling . . . pushing him along into the end zone."

That 64-yard run by the rookie from Boston College set up a 24-16 victory and the first postseason appearance for the Browns after their return in 1999. It was the last playoff appearance until 2020.

In 2021, there was Nick Chubb's 70-yard touchdown run in Cincinnati with Donovan saying Chubb was running in the direction of the Ohio River.

"There goes Chubb," said Donovan. "To the 35 . . . to the 40 . . . he's headed to the river!"

"Is he in the river yet?" yelled Dieken as Chubb crossed the goal line.

"He's in the river!" said Donovan.

The Browns loved those calls and the sheer joy Donovan brought to the games.

"They talk about next-level preparation for coaches and players. Jimmy did the same thing," said Browns senior vice president of communications Peter John-Baptiste, who stressed there is a "special relationship" between the head coach and play-by-play man. By the end of the week, the coach has done several interviews. He's tired. He's feeling the pressure of the upcoming game.

"Jimmy brought a level of professionalism and comfort," said John-Baptiste. "The coaches trusted him. They knew he was prepared. They appreciated that he was not like some new-school broadcasters who try to be bigger than the game."

Or as Knott said: "Jimmy Donovan didn't make it all about Jimmy Donovan."

That is one of the best compliments a radio play-by-play man can receive.

JOHNNY MANZIEL— SERIOUSLY?

They like shiny objects.

That's what I think about the Browns under the ownership of Jimmy Haslam, who took over the team in 2012.

"We've never been afraid to take big swings on things we think can help the team and help the organization," general manager Andrew Berry said in 2022 after the Deshaun Watson deal had totally collapsed. "Sometimes you'll hit, and sometimes they won't go quite according to plan . . . With any business where you take on risk or where you make decisions, you understand that there is both upside and downside. There's no such thing as a riskless transaction."

That's true—every trade, every draft pick, every signing comes with risk.

But how well does the risk match the possible reward? That's been a problem for the Browns since Haslam took over. Three of their biggest swings were drafting Johnny Manziel (2014) and trading for Odell Beckham Jr. (2019) and Deshaun Watson (2022). Those are the three riskiest moves since the franchise returned in 1999.

* * *

By the time the 2014 draft came along, Cleveland had shuffled through 20 quarterbacks since drafting Tim Couch to be the new franchise's first QB.

That's 20 quarterbacks in 15 years.

That's 20 quarterbacks, including names such as Doug Pederson (later a Super Bowl winning coach with Philadelphia), Ken Dorsey (later the Browns' offensive coordinator in 2024) and Trent Dilfer (who won a Super Bowl as a quarterback in Baltimore).

Before the 2014 draft, Couch had the most starts with 59. Then came Derek Anderson (34), Colt McCoy (21), Brandon Weeden (20), Charlie Frye (19), Brian Hoyer (16), Brady Quinn (12), Trent Dilfer (11) and Jeff Garcia (10). There are more names, but I stopped the list at those who made at least 10 starts. Those who started only once? Thad Lewis, Spergon Wynn and Bruce Gradkowski,

Remember, this is just the list of quarterbacks headed into the 2014 draft.

It illustrates the dismal dirge that has been the soundtrack of this franchise since 1999: Can't the Browns ever find a quarterback?

Which brings us to Johnny Manziel.

Where to start?

Some Browns fans remember the story of Jimmy Haslam and the "homeless guy." ESPN's Sal Paolantonio said he spent about 30 minutes with Haslam after Manziel was drafted, and Haslam told him: "I can go out to dinner anywhere in Tennessee and nobody bothers me . . . Here in Cleveland, everywhere I go, people know me. I was out to dinner recently and a homeless person was out on the street. He looked up at me and said, 'Draft Manziel.' "

Paolantonio said, "That convinced him that the Cleveland Browns fans wanted Manziel."

Haslam meant it as a funny story.

Paolantonio was not claiming Haslam was taking the advice of anyone on the street when it came to the draft. But after Manziel flamed out after 14 games in two seasons, this became yet another part of the draft night story that looked bad for Haslam and the Browns.

Manziel was a star at Texas A&M and a favorite of many fans who watched SEC football. Haslam, a Tennessee native and supporter of the University of Tennessee Vols, watches SEC football. He was probably watching as the 6-foot Manziel scrambled around, finding receivers open downfield — and fired reckless, daring but often successful passes. He also ran for touchdowns, putting an exclamation point on these dashes by diving headfirst into the end zone.

That's the superficial explanation for why the Browns selected Manziel with the 22nd pick in the 2014 draft. The owner wanted him. The marketing and sales department wanted him, too, especially team president Alec Scheiner. Most fans wanted him.

All of that was true.

But there was more.

So much more.

During the 2013 season, CEO Joe Banner was looking forward to the 2014 draft.

He had 10 picks—including two in the first round thanks to the Trent Richardson trade with the Colts. He had about $55 million in salary cap room. He had hired an outside analytics firm to study the quarterbacks in the 2014 draft. He also had his own analytics people with the Browns doing so.

Assistant general manager Ray Farmer and other scouts were sent across the country.

Banner was determined not to allow the Browns to draft Manziel.

"The day I was fired, Johnny Manziel was off our draft board," Banner told me.

At that point—Feb. 13, 2014—Banner's analytics team and scouts had ranked the top two quarterbacks in the 2014 draft as Louisville's Teddy Bridgewater and Fresno State's Derek Carr.

Two analytics reports had different ratings for the other quarterbacks. Some people in the front office preferred Carr, some Bridgewater. Other names coming up were Blake Bortles and Jimmy Garoppolo.

Banner had uncovered disturbing information about Manziel's personal problems at Texas A&M.

"We knew everything. I mean . . . everything," Banner told me.

Some of it wasn't hard to find out. A Sports Illustrated story had reported about Manziel's drinking and other issues. Basic scouting led to reports of Manziel not working hard in practice, showing up late for meetings, failing to take his job seriously. The Browns also had reports that Manziel's body was breaking down from hard hits he took in college.

"It was hard to believe he was going to hold up physically," said Banner. "We didn't think he looked that smart on the field. We didn't think he looked that accurate when passing. He didn't stay in the pocket very long . . ."

Some stats showed Manziel completing 75% of his passes from the pocket. However, Manziel was one of quickest quarterbacks in college football to leave the pocket.

In other words, when he threw from the pocket, he could be effective. But he hated throwing from the pocket because he was afraid of being sacked. Listed at 6-foot, he also had trouble seeing over taller linemen.

"My goal was for us to come out of the draft with a quarterback," said Banner. "It was either going to be Bridgewater or Carr. And if you look at what happened, when it came time for the Browns to use their second pick in the first round—both [players] were there."

* * *

So what happened?

Haslam's first mistake was firing Banner after Banner had helped lead the draft research.

Haslam's next mistake was promoting Ray Farmer, who was not

ready to be the general manager. Banner told Haslam that on the day he was fired. Banner stressed he liked Farmer. He had brought Farmer to the Browns from Kansas City, promoting him to assistant general manager. At some point, Farmer would be ready to be a general manager—but not yet. Banner would have been willing to allow Farmer to replace Michael Lombardi as general manager.

Haslam didn't care. At the age of 39, Farmer became the NFL's second-youngest general manager when he was promoted by Haslam.

Farmer had been a star at Duke and played three years (32 games) as a linebacker with the Philadelphia Eagles. A major knee injury led to an early retirement. Farmer worked in the scouting departments for Atlanta and Kansas City from 2002 to 2012 before coming to the Browns in 2013. He was building the right background to eventually become a general manager. But the odds were stacked outrageously against him when Haslam flung him into the job and paired him with a rookie head coach—when both men were strangers to each other.

There's something else about Farmer that led to Manziel becoming the Browns' quarterback. Farmer was an old-style football man. He believed in building teams on the lines—offense and defense. (His best draft pick in 2014 was guard Joel Bitonio.)

He thought a team with a strong defense and a respectable running game could overcome the lack of a star quarterback.

I had several conversations with Farmer after he became general manager. He wasn't a fool. He knew the Browns needed a franchise-changing quarterback. But he didn't see one in the 2014 draft. He also didn't believe in drafting wide receivers high, or spending a lot of money in free agency to sign them.

It's unfair to say Farmer considered the quarterback just another position on the field. But he thought many quarterbacks were interchangeable parts. That's an important point. I was told Farmer scouted Manziel personally. He had major doubts about

Browns fans go cuckoo for Johnny Football on draft night. The feeling would not last long. *John Kuntz / The Plain Dealer*

Manziel's NFL future. I also was told by someone close to the Browns that Farmer liked University of Louisville quarterback Teddy Bridgewater. But Bridgewater had a dismal performance at a pro day workout organized by the school to showcase his talent. The coaches and scouts had major concerns. Farmer began to feel alone in his support for Bridgewater, and even he was shocked by how poorly Bridgewater threw that day.

Farmer was trying to form some type of consensus regarding a quarterback. Offensive coordinator Kyle Shanahan liked Jimmy Garoppolo. There was some support for Derek Carr, some for Manziel.

With Banner gone, it was easier for the pro-Manziel voices to become louder. Quarterback coach Dowell Loggains was a Manziel fan. It's unclear where head coach Mike Pettine stood on Manziel. I sense he was a little like Farmer—not willing to stand up to the

Manziel tidal wave that was emanating from the owner's suite and elsewhere.

The $100,000 Banner spent on the outside research combined with the Browns' own analytics had put a metaphorical big red *X* through the name of Manziel. But Farmer was rooted in traditional football and had little interest in analytics. He was not ready to pound the table and demand any quarterback in the 2014 draft be picked by the Browns. He didn't feel strongly about any of them.

* * *

It's fascinating to look at the 2014 scouting reports on Manziel from the "draft experts" in print and online media.

Here's how ESPN's Mel Kiper ranked the top seven quarterbacks on his final "big board" on the eve of the draft:

1. Johnny Manziel
2. Blake Bortles
3. Derek Carr
4. Teddy Bridgewater
5. Tom Savage
6. A.J. McCarron
7. Jimmy Garoppolo

On April 25, according to Athlon Sports, in an article by Braden Gall, Kiper had Bridgewater at No.1, followed by Bortles and then Manziel, Carr, Garoppolo and McCarron.

Another well-known analyst at the time was Mike Mayock of NFL.com. He later became the general manager of the Las Vegas Raiders. He ranked the quarterbacks this way before the draft:

1. Manziel
2. Bortles
3. Carr

4. Garoppolo
5. Bridgewater

ESPN.com's Todd McShay is also well known for his draft research. His ratings were:

1. Bortles
2. Bridgewater
3. Manziel
4. Garoppolo

A reporter for Pro Football Weekly, Nolan Nawrocki, was not caught up in the Manziel hype. Nawrocki wrote that Manziel had "suspect intangibles . . . he carries a sense of entitlement and prima donna arrogance . . . [He] is known to party too much and is drawn to all the trappings of the game."

The fantasy website WalterFootball, run by Walter Cherepinsky, also had doubts about Manziel, ranking him the ninth best quarterback prospect in 2014. It was by far the lowest ranking Manziel got from any of the 12 sites compiled by Athlon's Gall.

WalterFootball reporter Charlie Campbell said in 2014 that Manziel's weaknesses included "off-the-field concerns; focus on football; likes to party; celebrity lifestyle."

Campbell cited Manziel as "probably the most high-profile and debated prospect since Tim Tebow in the 2010 NFL draft." He said there are "scouts and coaches who feel torn about whether the positives or negatives are going to win out during his (Manziel's) NFL career. Adding to the doubts is Manziel's party lifestyle and questions whether he will be focused enough on football during his career."

Campbell noted that at Texas A&M, Manziel was "bailed out" by the play of receiver Mike Evans and he was the beneficiary of "some phenomenal offensive line talent."

Campbell concluded by writing that some "quarterback-needy teams . . . plan to pass on Manziel [in the draft] because they don't feel he can be trusted off the field. They wonder how he's going to respond to the money and celebrity lifestyle of an NFL quarterback."

So, Nawrocki and WalterFootball had doubts. But what about all the others? As it turned out, Mel Kiper and "the homeless guy" were wrong, wrong, wrong.

For what it's worth, I wrote not one but two columns pleading with the Browns not to draft Manziel. Like Banner, I disliked the college offensive system he had played in. It's the chaotic style of never taking snaps under center and no significant playbook. Before many games, he was given 10-12 basic play sets to run and then was free to improvise.

* * *

Farmer took an odd approach to the 2014 draft, especially considering the fact that he was so new to the job. The general manager skipped the pro day workouts of Manziel, Bridgewater, Bortles and other top prospects. (He did watch video tapes of those workouts.) Also, the Browns did not interview the highest rated quarterbacks at the scouting combine—where most teams try to do just that.

"A pro day of orchestrated throws, I don't know what that tells you," Farmer told several media people who cover the Browns.

He had a point. During those skill showcases the quarterback is in shorts and a shirt. A receiver goes out for passes. No one rushes the quarterback or covers the receiver. The point is to display the quarterback's arm strength and accuracy. It's kind of like watching a basketball player practice 3-point shots—alone in the gym.

But at least you can see if the player is moving as if he's healthy. You can talk to people at the school where the pro day is held. It's the player's school.

Still, it's a small part of the evaluation process.

Farmer told the media in 2014 that attending pro days "is a piece of it that people blow up into this great thing. I went to a lot of games and practices. I've seen them throw the ball."

Pettine also skipped a lot of those workouts.

For Browns fans, those choices brought up questions. Why isn't Farmer doing the same basic work of most general managers? Farmer explained the top quarterbacks were coming to the team training complex in Berea to work out and meet with the Browns for private visits.

I remember thinking, *None of this will matter if the Browns have a good draft. But if they don't, it will count against Farmer.*

Well, the 2014 draft went badly.

Very badly for the Browns—and Farmer.

When the pressure to take Manziel built in the draft room, Farmer was not able to fight it off. Ownership and others wanted to give Manziel a chance. Farmer went along with the flow.

Quarterback coach Dowell Loggains made things even worse for his new front office after the draft when he gave an interview with radio host Bo Mattingly on Arkansas ESPN. Loggains, one of the pre-draft supporters of Manziel, said he was texting Manziel during the draft.

"We were sitting there and they kept showing Johnny on TV," Loggains told Mattingly. "Johnny shoots me a text and says, 'I wish you guys would come get me. Hurry up and draft me because I want to be there. I want to wreck this league together.' When I got that text, I forwarded it to the owner and the head coach."

According to Loggains, he received this text from Haslam:

" 'Pull the trigger, we're trading up to get this guy.' "

Someone who knows what happened told me the Browns had already traded their No. 26 pick (the draft pick they had received in the Trent Richardson trade) and a third-round pick to Philadelphia for the No. 22 pick. The Browns were convinced that Kansas City, which had the 23rd pick, wanted to draft Manziel.

When their turn came, the Browns called Manziel's name.

The Loggains interview made it look even worse for Farmer, as if he was absent during the decision-making. I happen to think Loggains was creating his own scenario so that he could be a part of the process of drafting Manziel, and I'm not sure all his details were accurate. But it made the Browns appear disorganized when he told the story to the radio host, who was his friend.

"It shows you how competitive this kid is," Loggains added in the radio interview. "I got to spend so much time with him leading up to this process. I feel like I know him very well . . . He has a chip on his shoulder and he wants to be a Brown."

Manziel went on the draft-night stage, rubbed his fingers together in the money sign and put on a Browns cap. Fans and most members of the media were gleeful.

In the post-draft press conference, Farmer explained that the Browns decided to pursue Manziel "in the middle of the draft [first round]. We took the opportunity to take players in the order we had them ranked."

I can give you a lot of other quotes from Farmer about drafting Manziel, but they are just generalities.

Pettine, immediately after becoming head coach in January 2014, had talked about wanting players "who play like a Brown." He meant they were tough, unselfish and hard-working.

Did that fit Manziel?

"We liked his ability to perform and make plays," Farmer said on draft night. "We liked a guy that brought all those things when we talked about 'play like a Brown.' He was passionate. He was relentless. He played fearlessly."

At Texas A&M, Manziel was known as a poor practice player. He wasn't a quarterback who loved to study scouting reports and video of opponents. An ESPN magazine story had his father saying he worried Manziel was an alcoholic. There were other huge question marks next to Manziel in the "play like a Brown" category that the new regime was selling.

Pettine said "playing like a Brown" was "passion, competitive, being tough mentally and physically . . . being accountable . . . it's a list of intangibles. It's not how high they jump. It's not athletic ability . . . when we say, 'He plays like a Brown,' that's the biggest compliment you can give."

Pettine also talked about how Manziel had the "it" factor.

"His 'It' factor is at an extreme level," Pettine said. "It's to the point where it's really created 'Johnny Football.' He has all those things to an amazing degree. He's ultra-competitive, ultra-passionate . . . he's just a guy who finds a way."

That's what Farmer and Pettine found themselves saying about Manziel on draft night.

* * *

The next day—right before Manziel appeared at the Browns' facility in Berea for a press conference—ESPN reported that Browns' star receiver Josh Gordon had failed another drug test. It was likely he'd be out for the season.

This was something Banner had feared.

In the middle of the 2013 season, he had a deal set up to trade Gordon to San Francisco for a second-round pick. The coaches were adamantly against it. Gordon was on his way to a Pro Bowl season. Haslam had no interest in trading him. The Browns decided to gamble that Gordon would stay clean and pass his tests.

But sometime after the 2013 season, Gordon was tested and failed. The league didn't announce the results, but someone leaked it (bad pun) to ESPN right after the Browns drafted Manziel. My understanding is the front office was aware of Gordon's failed test before the first round of the 2014 draft. That didn't lead Farmer to change direction and draft a receiver. Remember his philosophy of finding receivers lower in the draft.

Banner watched the draft and couldn't believe what had happened. As he told me years later, "When they drafted Manziel, I nearly fell off the couch."

But Browns fans stood and cheered. And they bought 1,500

season tickets within 12 hours of Manziel's name being called. After two days, it was 2,300 season tickets. Browns jerseys with Manziel's name were quickly produced and sold briskly.

This would be the highlight of Manziel's two seasons with the Browns.

* * *

Manziel was a disaster with the Browns.

In 2014, the starting quarterback was Brian Hoyer, a Cleveland area native. A former New England Patriot, Hoyer made the NFL as an undrafted player out of Michigan State. Cleveland players had enormous respect for Hoyer. Most of them viewed Manziel with disdain because of the rookie's sense of entitlement.

Manziel gave a revealing interview in 2024 with former NFL star Shannon Sharpe on his podcast. One of the people he blamed for his failure in Cleveland was Hoyer.

"My quarterback room was not a home for me because of Brian Hoyer . . . He had been waiting for an opportunity to really provide for his family . . . He saw how much of an upper hand he had on me, and he didn't hold back when it came to that."

There was a culture clash between the two quarterbacks. Manziel oozed entitlement. Hoyer, who had grown up in the Cleveland suburb of North Olmsted, had the working-class mentality of Northeast Ohio.

Manziel expected to be given the starting quarterback job because of what he did in college.

Hoyer knew nothing would ever be simply handed to him on the football field. During his senior year at Cleveland St. Ignatius High, Hoyer had to wait in the recruiting season to land an offer from Michigan State. Former St. Ignatius coach Chuck Kyle was begging big-time schools to sign his quarterback.

"Michigan State was one of the few programs that saw what Brian could do," Kyle told me in a 2020 interview. "You need an

Fans wanted to believe . . . but Johnny Manziel proved to be a disaster for the Browns. *Joshua Gunter / The Plain Dealer*

offense where your quarterback drops back to pass and can throw downfield. You need a strong running game. It's more a pro style."

At Michigan State, Hoyer waited two years to become a starter. In the 2009 NFL draft, he wasn't selected. He made the Patriots roster as an undrafted free agent. He was in the same quarterback room as Tom Brady. Hoyer was trained in the Patriot Way. You came to work to . . . well . . . work. You take home game videos and other football material to study. You also know you can be replaced when you're Brady's backup. Coach Bill Belichick was demanding when it came to preparation. Brady had the same mindset. If you fail to do your homework and are not ready, you sometimes are humiliated. Hoyer did three different tours of duty with New England because of his work ethic and serious approach.

Hoyer also had a 10-6 record as a starter with the Browns.

Manziel was "Johnny Football" even in high school. He received

Some Browns players said that when Johnny Manziel finally did get on the field, it was clear he didn't have a solid grasp of the offense.
Joshua Gunter / The Plain Dealer

far more recruiting attention than Hoyer. As a freshman at Texas A&M, Manziel won the Heisman Trophy.

"I felt like the harder I partied, the better I played," Manziel told Sharpe. "I'd go to the walk-throughs at 10 in the morning smelling like a liquor store."

Manziel had no clue how, with the Browns, his arrogance would create a division between himself and his new teammates.

Manziel also told Sharpe: "There were instances in the quarterback room early on where I would ask the same question a couple of times, and he [Hoyer] would be at the head of the table and go, 'Pfft, again? We're doing this again? Keep him out of it. Cut that off.' And I don't have a bad word to say about Brian Hoyer. That is just a fact of what happened in that room."

If that's all Hoyer said, it was extremely mild compared to how the Patriots and several other teams treat players who aren't prepared.

Hoyer responded later during an appearance on the NFL Network's "Good Morning Football":

> Johnny's right. That was an opportunity for me to go out and be the starter for my hometown team, but I was kind of apathetic towards him . . . I didn't go out of my way to be a jerk to him. But I was trying to win this job and go out and perform the best I could. I feel sorry that he feels that way about it . . . I never had any animosity toward Johnny. If anything, it was towards the owner and the GM who were always trying to push him ahead of me when clearly he wasn't ready and I was gonna be the starter. It's unfortunate that that left a bad taste in his mouth . . . I feel bad that he feels that way.

Hall of Fame left tackle Joe Thomas and others with the Browns said when Manziel finally did get on the field, it was clear he didn't have a solid grasp of the offense. The Browns players didn't care what Manziel had done in college. They needed a quarterback who was a dedicated professional to help them win—not a guy who still thought life was a party.

Manziel's NFL career covered two seasons. He was 2-6 as a starter. He was paid $5.5 million during his tenure.

About the only good part of this story is the fact that the cost of the Manziel deal was much less than later deals for Deshaun Watson and Odell Beckham Jr. The Browns traded their No. 26 and 83rd picks in the 2014 draft to move up to No. 22 and take Manziel.

That should have been a warning sign. No. 22 is a bad draft spot for Cleveland quarterbacks since the Browns returned in 1999. The others picked at that spot were Brady Quinn (2007) and Brandon Weeden (2012). Neither had notable Cleveland careers.

SEARCHING AND SEARCHING: THE DRAFT

Drafting Johnny Manziel helped lead to the eventual firing of GM Ray Farmer and head coach Mike Pettine. So did another awful decision in the 2014 draft—selecting defensive back Justin Gilbert, with the No. 8 overall pick. That was 14 spots ahead of Manziel.

Gilbert played 23 games in two years for the Browns, making only three starts. He was traded to Pittsburgh before the 2016 session. There, he appeared in 12 games, none as a starter. Gilbert then was suspended for the 2017 season by the NFL for violating the league's drug policy. He never played in the NFL again.

Manziel appeared in 14 games, eight as a starter—all with Cleveland. His last NFL season was 2015.

The two Ray Farmer drafts (2014 and 2015) and a 4-12 record in 2015 led Browns owner Jimmy Haslam to do what he tended to do best in those early days of his tenure—fire people.

Consider the following:

2012: Haslam bought the team when the season opened. The sale was approved by the NFL after the Browns played their sixth game. Haslam inherited Mike Holmgren as president, Tom Heckert as GM and Pat Shurmur as head coach. All were fired by the end of the season. The team's record was 5-11.

2013: CEO Joe Banner was part of the Haslam group taking over. Banner hired Mike Lombardi as the GM. Rob Chudzinski was the new coach. They had a 4-12 record. Chudzinski was fired at the end of the season. Two months later, Banner and Lombardi were fired.

2014–15: This was the Farmer/Pettine regime. They had records of 7-9 and then 3-13. Two years and they were gone.

2016: A desperate Haslam decided to try something different—a pure analytics approach, a football version of baseball's Moneyball. Sashi Brown was promoted to executive vice president, which is similar to GM. Andrew Berry was named vice president of player personnel, much like assistant GM. The most interesting hire was Paul DePodesta, the former baseball GM. He was one of the architects of baseball's Moneyball approach when working for Billy Beane with the Oakland A's. The Browns' new head coach was Hue Jackson, whose last job was offensive coordinator with the Cincinnati Bengals.

Haslam went from traditional football guys (Holmgren and Heckert) to an early advocate of analytics (Banner) to a traditional football guy (Farmer) to the most ambitious analytics approach in the NFL up to that time (Brown).

All of that in five football seasons.

* * *

With the new front office in place and lots of new plans, the Browns entered the 2016 draft with the No. 2 pick.

Their favorite player was Jared Goff, the quarterback from California. However, Tennessee had the first pick in the draft, and when the Titans traded it to the Rams, it was clear Goff was L.A.'s target.

That left Carson Wentz as a possible quarterback selection. He played at North Dakota State, where he started 23 games. The Browns were not overly impressed with Wentz or any other quarterback in that draft besides Goff. Once it was clear Goff was gone, they decided to trade the No. 2 pick.

Philadelphia wanted Wentz. The Browns shipped the No. 2 pick and a future pick (it became the 139th pick in the 2017 draft) to the Eagles.

In return, they received picks No. 8, 77 and 100 in the 2016 draft. They also received what became the No. 12 pick in 2017 and a second-round pick in 2018.

Suppose the Browns had just stopped there. Here's a list of the key players who were picked at those spots:

No. 8: Tackle Jack Conklin. He later signed with Cleveland and has been an excellent Pro Bowl caliber player.

No. 76: Tackle Shon Coleman, whom the Browns kept.

2017 First-rounder: Quarterback Deshaun Watson, No. 12 eventually traded to Houston.

That's right, the Browns could have had Conklin and Watson at this point, assuming they picked the same players taken in those spots.

But the Browns kept trading and trading. They were like someone who had thrown quarters into a slot machine and hit the 7s . . . Jackpot! As a tidal wave of quarters rumbled out of the machine, the Browns kept scooping them up and throwing them back into the machine.

Casinos count on gamblers who win to keep gambling until . . . in the end . . . they lose.

The Browns shipped that No. 8 pick from the Eagles to Tennessee for more picks. They received a first-round pick in 2016 (No. 15) and a second-round pick in 2017.

This stuff can drive you nuts but in the end, here's what the Browns had to show for all those deals:

First-rounders: Corey Coleman (2016), Jabrill Peppers (2017) and Denzel Ward (2018).

Other players who came to the Browns in those series of deals via the draft: Cody Kessler, Derrick Kindred, Spencer Drango, Ricardo Louis and Jordan Payton.

The Browns had 14 selections in the 2016 draft. The best player they picked was defensive end Emmanuel Ogbah (played nine years). Others of note were linebacker Joe Schobert (played seven years), receiver Rashard Higgins (played seven years) and defensive end Carl Nassib (played seven years). None were stars.

* * *

The 2016 draft was not just analytics driven, it was analytics to the extreme. Sports Illustrated's Jenny Vrentas wrote this the day after the 2016 Browns draft:

> Hue Jackson and Paul DePodesta emerged from the Browns' draft room together, wearing matching team pins on the left lapel of their suit jackets. They had just drafted their first player in Cleveland, speedy Baylor receiver Corey Coleman, and they looked quite pleased. Not just because Coleman was the top player on their board at a position of need, but because they had also executed their master plan, perhaps even better than expected. Imagine that, the "football guy" and the "Moneyball guy," on the same page.
>
> "I know everybody is watching us, and rightfully so, and they can," Jackson said. "I said on Day One, we are going to be on the cutting edge of what we do. Well, we showed a piece of that the other day. I'm sure people will say, how did they make this happen, like you are asking right now. We have a plan, and we are working The Plan. And we are very happy, for our first time out, to produce the way we did.

Vrentas admitted, "It's unwise to overreact to any draft right after it ends, because it will take a few years to know whether the players selected were hits or misses."

But she was impressed with how the Browns kept piling up the draft picks:

They turned their No. 2 overall pick, via two trades down in the first round with Philadelphia and Tennessee, into this haul: the No. 15 pick, two third-rounders, a fourth-rounder, a 2017 first- and second-rounder and a 2018 second-rounder (they also gave up a sixth-round pick and a future fourth). That's stunning. Overall, Cleveland made five trades to turn 10 draft picks into 14 rookies, 2017 first- and second-round picks, a 2018 second-rounder and veteran cornerback Jamar Taylor. That's 15 new players who can try to plug holes on a depleted roster. And then there's next year, which is, as DePodesta put it, "in effect, it is two drafts."

I also bought into the Mr. Big Volume approach to the draft.

My story ran under the headline of "Cleveland Browns Draft is Reason for Hope with Seven All-Americans, Four Receivers and 14 Players."

My thought was that out of 14 guys, the Browns had to find a few players. At least one or two of them should make a Pro Bowl.

I thought wrong.

Far too many premature victory laps were being taken after that 2016 draft by those who loved the approach but forgot that old-fashioned scouting and player evaluation was needed. Having all those picks only matters if you pick the right guys.

In retrospect, the Browns could have kept that No. 2 pick and selected among future stars such as Joey Bosa, Jalen Ramsey, Tyreek Hill and Michael Thomas.

If they wanted a quarterback, they could have selected a better one than Wentz. Dallas found Mississippi State's Dak Prescott in the fourth round. He made three Pro Bowls. That's right, three Pro Bowls for a fourth-rounder.

Here's the part that really hurts: The Browns drafted these players before Prescott was drafted at No: 135 . . .

No. 15: Corey Coleman.
No. 32: Emmanuel Ogbah.
No. 65 Carl Nassib.
No. 76 Shon Coleman.
No. 91: Cody Kessler.
No. 99 Joe Schobert.
No. 114: Ricardo Louis.

Yikes! The Browns went for a quarterback in the third round—Kessler, who had a very weak throwing arm.

Before the draft, ESPN's Mel Kiper ranked Prescott as the No. 114 best player available. After the Cowboys selected Prescott, Kiper wrote:

> Dallas was interested in getting into range for Paxton Lynch and also missed out on a chance to draft Connor Cook when the Raiders traded up. Dak Prescott is a solid guy to have on the bench, but I question the starting upside . . .

The Browns weren't the only team to miss on Prescott in this draft and select another quarterback.

Here are the quarterbacks picked before Prescott, with where they were drafted and how many NFL starts they had made entering the 2025 season:

No. 1: Jared Goff, Rams. 134 starts.
No. 2: Carson Wentz, Eagles. 94 starts.
No. 26: Paxton Lynch, Broncos. Four starts.
No. 51: Christian Hackenberg, Jets. Zero starts.
No. 91: Jacoby Brissett, Patriots. 53 starts.
No. 93: Cody Kessler, Browns. 12 starts.
No. 100: Connor Cook, Raiders. Zero starts.
No. 135: Dak Prescott, Cowboys. 122 starts.

As for the Browns draft, Kiper gave it a "C." He wasn't impressed by many of the selections. He called Kessler "a stretch in the third round" and didn't consider the USC product a future NFL starter.

Kessler did play three years in the NFL, but had a 2-10 record as a starter.

A bigger disaster was Coleman. The receiver also had a three-year NFL career, covering 27 games. He caught 56 passes, five for TDs. He suffered a broken hand and other injuries.

What a mess.

NO ONE WILL THANK SASHI BROWN, BUT THEY SHOULD

"Don't you realize what the Browns just did?" An NFL executive was almost screaming at me on the phone. "They just paid $16 million for a second pick. It's just stupid."

The executive was talking about a deal the Browns made March 9, 2017. The Houston Texans had been calling nearly every team in the NFL, trying to dump quarterback Brock Osweiler and his $16 million salary for the 2017 season. Cleveland was near the top of their list because the Browns always seemed to be in the market for a quarterback—even a bad one.

Osweiler had a 13-8 career record as a starter, but the Texans often won in spite of him. He was neither an accurate passer (16 interceptions compared to 15 TD passes) nor an athletic runner.

The Browns didn't care about that. They had marginal interest in Osweiler. But the front office, led by executive vice president Sashi Brown, had another idea. Their plan was utterly new to the NFL. It was why owner Jimmy Haslam promoted Brown. It also was why Brown hired former MLB executive Paul DePodesta and gave him the title of chief strategy officer. It was an analytics driven proposal.

The Browns asked themselves, *Is it worth paying $16 million for a second-round pick?*

Cleveland Browns owner Jimmy Haslam (left) and executive vice president of football operations Sashi Brown talk before a game in 2017.
John Kuntz / cleveland.com

In the spring of 2017 the Browns were coming off a 1-15 season. They were in "asset accumulation" mode. And the main assets they wanted were draft picks.

The Browns also had about $100 million in salary cap room.

"We'll take Osweiler, but give us draft picks, too," they said.

I'm sure they asked for a first-round choice. Houston wasn't willing to do that. But the Texans desperately wanted to remove Osweiler from the salary cap. No other team had any interest in him unless the Texans would take an expensive contract on a bad player in return.

Cleveland was their only option.

Houston sent Osweiler, plus a second-round pick in 2018 and a sixth-round pick in 2017, to the Browns for a fourth-round pick in 2017.

"Houston's long sports nightmare is over now that the Texans have traded underperforming quarterback Brock Osweiler to Cleveland . . . " the Houston Chronicle's Craig Hlavaty reported. Houston's "long nightmare" was actually one season. The deal was greeted in Houston with applause for the home team. It was worth a second-round pick to get Osweiler off the salary cap.

Meanwhile, the Browns' analytics team had lots of data about second-round picks. It showed that more than 90% of second-round picks remained on the team for at least two years. Close to 40% started for more than two years. All of those players were on the salary cap–friendly rookie contracts.

Paying $16 million for a second-round pick when you have millions and millions in salary cap room? Why not?

Many people in the NFL and in the media were confused.

I knew exactly what the Browns were doing because I had watched the Cavs make the same type of trade in 2011. The Cavs sent Mo Williams and Jamario Moon to the L.A. Clippers for an overpriced and overweight Baron Davis—and insisted that the Clippers add a first-round draft pick to the deal.

By the time all the contracts changed teams, the Cavs gained about $30 million in cash and salary cap space with Davis—who would be released in the summer of 2011. Cavs GM Chris Grant insisted the Clippers add an "unprotected" first round pick in 2011 to the package.

That 2011 draft was the year the Cavs picked Kyrie Irving. They won the NBA draft lottery despite the Clippers' ball (now theirs) having only a 2.8% chance of being selected No. 1.

Bottom line: They basically bought a future All-Star guard for the $30 million contract that belonged to Baron Davis.

I explained all this to the NFL executive, who didn't fully understand the thinking. He still thought $16 million was an outrageous price for a second-round pick.

It would be 14 months from the time of the Osweiler trade in 2017 until the 2018 draft when the Browns would have that second-round pick. By then, the man behind the deal was long gone. Sashi Brown was fired and replaced with John Dorsey.

In the 2018 draft, the Browns had the top pick in the second round—No. 33 overall. That was their own pick. The Houston pick for which they traded was No. 35.

With that 33rd selection, the Browns picked offensive lineman Austin Corbett. He started only one game in 1½ seasons with the Browns. General manager John Dorsey was discouraged about the lack of playing time for Corbett. He believed the coaching staff wasn't giving Corbett a chance. So Dorsey traded Corbett to the Rams, on Oct. 15, 2019, for a 2021 fifth-round pick. Corbett quickly became a starter for the Rams and later the Panthers.

With the 35th pick that came from Houston, Dorsey selected Nick Chubb. Browns fans know Chubb became one of the best running backs in Cleveland history.

And it happened because of a trade that few in the NFL were willing to make—except Sashi Brown.

Whatever happened to Brock Osweiler?

After being cut by the Browns, the Montana native played two more seasons, with Miami and Denver, having a 2-7 record as a starter for those two teams. His career ended at the age of 28.

This story does have a happy ending for Osweiler, who recreated himself as a college football analyst for ESPN. According to the website Overthecap.com, Osweiler was paid $41 million during his seven-year NFL career.

ANALYTICS: ON AND OFF AND ON AGAIN

The Browns ended their 2015 season with a 28-12 loss to Pittsburgh. Then, as usually happens after the Browns conclude a season with a loss to Pittsburgh—people were fired.

Before dealing with after the aftermath of the 2015 season, let's look at another Browns firing. This was back in 2008, right before the Browns were to end that season—in Pittsburgh.

Phil Savage had been the team's GM since 2005. In 2007, after the Browns went 10-6. Savage and head coach Romeo Crennel received lucrative contract extensions from owner Randy Lerner.

Then, the 2008 season was a nightmare of quarterback injuries, some players acting up, and the team losing. As the season wound down, after several talks with Lerner, Savage was under the impression he would remain with the Browns in 2009. Not so for Crennel. Savage had already put together a list of coaching candidates to replace him. With a few weeks left in the 2008 season, I had a serious discussion with Savage about Rex Ryan taking over as head coach in 2009. It sounded as if Ryan was at the top of Savage's list.

Savage also was scouting, with the 2009 draft coming up and the Browns certain to have a high first-round pick because of their woeful 2008 season.

The night before their final game in Pittsburgh, Savage was in the Charlotte airport, returning from a scouting trip. He received a call from Randy Lerner.

"I was fired over the phone while sitting in one of those rocking chairs in the airport," said Savage. "I still wondered if Randy was going to stick to his decision, so I went to the game in Pittsburgh anyway."

Why was Savage unsure if he had really been fired? Randy Lerner could see seven sides of a square. He could make a decision, then have someone change his mind. Savage decided to meet with Lerner in person and be told—face-to-face—that he was fired. He wasn't going to be written off on the phone in an airport.

I saw Savage at that Dec. 28, 2008, game in Pittsburgh. We talked for a bit. I could tell something was wrong. He didn't say much. At halftime, he told me that he'd touch base after the game. He did, and told me he had been fired. The team announced it about 15 minutes later.

Yes, Savage watched the game as the Browns' GM even though he was no longer the Browns' GM. He tried to have that in-person meeting with Lerner, but it never happened. A few weeks later, Eric Mangini was hired as head coach and to essentially serve as his own GM.

Back to 2015 . . .

As the Browns staggered to the end of another dreadful season, the Browns announced a press conference a few hours after their 28-12 loss to Pittsburgh. That loss made their final season record 3-13. For a few months, it had been expected that GM Ray Farmer and head coach Mike Pettine would be fired when the season was over. And they were.

But when the Browns announced that Sashi Brown would be in charge of football operations, many people in the media said . . . *Who?*

We knew Sashi Brown—he had been the Browns' salary cap

expert since 2013. But he was now being promoted from a specialist role to what amounted to the general manager position?

Indeed.

Owner Jimmy Haslam had bought the team in 2012. At the end of that season, he fired team president Mike Holmgren, GM Tom Heckert and head coach Pat Shurmur.

In 2013, he hired Joe Banner as CEO, Mike Lombardi as GM and Rob Chudzinski as head coach.

Well, that lasted a year.

And became another Pittsburgh firing story.

The Browns were ending the 2013 season against the Steelers—in what wound up a 20-7 loss. At halftime, word leaked out to media that Chudzinski would be fired after the game. Chudzinski's wife and friends heard the news on the TV halftime show. The coach, though, didn't find out until after the game as he was heading into the press conference. One of the Browns' public relations people told him to be prepared for questions about his rumored firing. Chudzinski told the media he knew nothing about it—which he didn't. He was informed after the press conference.

* * *

By 2016, Jimmy Haslam wanted to try something new. He had long been fascinated by statistical analysis. He used different forms of it in his Pilot/Flying J truck stop business. He also was interested in baseball's "Moneyball" approach and wondered if that numbers-driven strategy could be applied to football. Sashi Brown, who also had a background in business, believed that it could.

So Haslam put Brown in charge of the football operation.

He also hired former baseball "Moneyball" executive Paul DePodesta to help Sashi Brown change the way the Browns would do business. DePodesta came in with the title Chief Strategy Officer. He also would work with Haslam in some of the owner's other business interests.

The Browns already had their eye on Cincinnati offensive coordinator Hue Jackson to be their next head coach—starting with the 2016 season. And they did hire Jackson, although DePodesta preferred Sean McDermott.

Ownership has the final say on hiring coaches, Joe Banner once told me. Sometimes owners go along with the recommendations of their executives. Other times, owners pick their own coaches. Haslam, during his ownership, has done both.

Jackson was one of his guys.

Sashi Brown and DePodesta explained to Haslam their idea: Rip up the roster, lose a lot of games, and add draft picks.

Brown told me not long after he was promoted that the Browns had the most expensive defense in the NFL. They had the 16th oldest roster. As usual, they had no quarterback. And they were coming off a 3-13 season.

He didn't use these words, but I will . . . *They blew it up.*

Veteran players were dumped. Salary cap space opened up as the roster became younger and cheaper. Trades were made with a goal of moving down in the draft, dealing a high pick for multiple picks in lower rounds. On the field, there was a tidal wave of losses. The team was 1-15 in 2016.

This strategy led to the first pick in the 2017 draft, which the Browns got right with Myles Garrett.

But the 2017 Browns still had no quarterback.

They kept losing and losing.

Jackson was feuding with Sashi Brown, claiming the front office didn't explain to him the strategy. Jackson believed he would be fired because of all the losses.

Owners Jimmy and Dee Haslam liked Jackson personally. They believed they had put the coach in a terrible position with a roster set up to lose. They also had lost faith in the Sashi Brown/analytics approach. Jackson was telling ownership these guys didn't know how to build a roster.

Media criticism was harsh, the main point being that a bunch of Ivy League graduates couldn't put together a football team. Sashi Brown had a law degree from Harvard. DePodesta graduated from Harvard. The team also had hired as GM Andrew Berry—another Harvard man.

On Dec. 4, 2017, the Browns lost 19-10 to the Chargers. That made their record 0-12 . . . and a total of 1-27 since the new analytics approach was installed.

Haslam couldn't take it anymore. On Dec. 7, 2017, he fired Sashi Brown. Twelve hours later, he announced the hiring of John Dorsey as the new GM.

* * *

When Haslam purchased the team, with Joe Banner as his CEO, Haslam liked Banner's use of analytics. Banner had developed some of those concepts while president of the Philadelphia Eagles. He continued using them in Cleveland. If you look at his 2013 Browns draft, he traded down in a few rounds. He traded running back Trent Richardson early in the 2013 season to the Colts for a 2014 first-round pick. He had a trade set up to send talented but troubled receiver Josh Gordon for a future second-round pick, but ownership vetoed that one. They believed Gordon could get his drug problem under control. They were wrong.

Haslam became discontented with Banner and fired him after one year. Ray Farmer was promoted to GM. He was a former NFL linebacker, an old-school football guy. The new analytics is discarded.

Here's how it breaks down in the early Haslam years:

2012: After Haslam bought the Browns, Mike Holmgren and his front office are fired. They were old-school football guys.

2013: Joe Banner is hired. Analytics is introduced to the franchise.

2014: Banner is fired. No more analytics. Ray Farmer is old-school football.
2016: Farmer is replaced by Sashi Brown and Paul DePodesta, who bring in super-sized analytics.
2017: Brown is fired. John Dorsey is hired as the new GM on Dec. 7, 2017. Analytics is out.

Dorsey had played in the NFL. He was a pure scout/player personnel man, having spent 19 years in those jobs with Green Bay. In 2013, he was hired as Kansas City GM. From 2013 to 2016, the Chiefs had a 43-21 record. Dorsey was part of the front office that engineered a trade to move up in the 2017 draft to select Patrick Mahomes with the No. 10 pick.

But Dorsey was fired by Kansas City in June 2017. One of the criticisms at that time was that he was more of a scout/player personnel expert and lacked the overall management skills of a GM. Also, head coach Andy Reid had joined the Chiefs in 2013. He brought along a young executive with him from his previous head coaching job in Philadelphia. (Side note: Reid had been hired there by Joe Banner).

The executive was Brett Veach. He came to the Eagles in 2004 as a coaching intern under Reid. Over the years, Reid promoted him in Philadelphia. Then Veach joined Kansas City's front office, where he worked under Dorsey. Reid had more than the normal coach's power. When Kansas City's ownership became disgruntled with Dorsey, it was an easy decision to fire him and promote Veach.

* * *

By the middle of the 2017 season, Haslam was looking to replace Sashi Brown. Dorsey was out of work, and he has a lot of friends and advocates in the NFL. Haslam was talking to Dorsey for more than a month before he replaced Sashi Brown on Dec. 7, 2017.

Dorsey was given a four-year contract and complete control of the roster, but there was one condition . . . Jackson had to return as coach in 2018. Dorsey quickly agreed.

Dorsey was excited to be back running a team. He knew the Browns had two first-round picks and two second-round picks in the 2018 draft. They had close to $100 million in salary cap room. (All due to the analytics approach.)

"John has been immersed in the NFL for 26 years, won two Super Bowls, built sustainable winning football teams and is highly respected for his football acumen," Haslam said of Dorsey's hiring. "We know we have a critical and very positive opportunity ahead of us to profoundly impact the foundation of this football team. Bringing in someone of John Dorsey's caliber, his track record of success and his experience, significantly strengthens our opportunities to build a winning football team and that has been, and continues to be, what we want for our fans."

Bottom line: Haslam didn't trust Sashi Brown and his staff with the enormous 2018 draft assets and salary cap room. He wanted a pure scout/talent evaluator to run that draft.

"Any personnel guy worth his weight would be excited," Dorsey said. "I'm not going to lie to you. I think Sashi did a nice job of creating some draft picks and creating some cap space here, but I'm excited. To me, this is an opportunity that not many personnel guys in my position would pass up."

That's what he said at his press conference.

A few weeks later, I asked him about Hue Jackson. He said some nice things about the coach, but quickly went back to all the draft picks and salary cap room in 2018. If he had to deal with Jackson in the short term, so be it. He'd worry about that later.

Here's part of what I wrote after Dorsey was hired:

> The Cleveland Browns wanted to hire an experienced general manager, and they found one in John Dorsey. They wanted a general manager who'd had success in turning around a fran-

chise. Dorsey did that in Kansas City, where they averaged nearly 11 wins over the previous four seasons.

By contrast, the Browns have won only 11 games in the last four years.

They also wanted a change from the analytics-based approach of Sashi Brown. That's also Dorsey. I'm still skeptical of owner Jimmy Haslam's decision to automatically wed Dorsey with coach Hue Jackson for the 2018 season. Both men are saying all the right things about that, admitting they also don't know each other.

I asked Dorsey about it being 'a prerequisite' that he work with Jackson.

He didn't answer that directly.

Instead, he said, "I like him as a man."

I asked, "What else?"

"I like the overall offensive schematic stuff," he said. "I think that's cool. They play hard. That symbolizes the AFC North. You have to play hard."

Of course, you have to play hard in any NFL division if you expect any degree of success.

That said, common sense says almost every general manager would prefer to hire his own coach rather than inherit one with a 1-31 record.

Owner Jimmy Haslam has also kept the chain of command chart the same: Jackson, Dorsey and chief strategy officer Paul DePodesta all report directly to ownership. In other words, the general manager is basically on the same level as the coach—although Dorsey will make the final decisions regarding the 53-man roster.

I prefer a general manager being over the coach. It could prevent some of the speculation that just happened in Berea, where indications are Jackson won a power struggle with Sashi Brown.

> Dorsey comes to town with more clout and a much longer football resume' than anyone else in the Browns football front office. That should give him clout. I hope they keep DePodesta and the best analytics people.
>
> I don't think analytics should drive the football bus. But it should have a spot in the front seat. Data, direction and an in-depth study of previous drafts, trades and salary cap structures are extremely helpful when trying to figure out what to do next.

Dorsey was assigned the job of finding a quarterback in the 2018 draft.

THEY GOT ONE RIGHT: PICKING MYLES GARRETT

The Browns should not have used their No. 1 pick in the 2017 draft on Myles Garrett.

What?

Garrett is going to be a Hall of Famer.

Taking a future Hall of Fame defensive end in a draft is never a mistake. It's the kind of move every GM dreams of making. Browns GM Sashi Brown had the No. 1 pick. He took the consensus No. 1 player in the 2017 draft—Garrett, from Texas A&M.

But if the Browns could go back in time and do it over again—or if any of the eight teams that drafted after the Browns in 2017 could do so—they would pick Patrick Mahomes instead. By the age of 29, Mahomes had led Kansas City to five Super Bowls. He was the No. 10 pick in the 2017 draft.

Before we look at how nearly everyone but the Chiefs missed on Mahomes, let's give credit to the Browns and Sashi Brown.

Right before the draft, I received a call from a well-known executive who was consulting for another NFL team.

"I keep hearing the Browns will take [Mitch] Trubisky," he said. "Is that true? Are they dumb enough to pass on Garrett?"

I started to say, "When it comes to the Browns and the draft, they are dumb enough to do almost anything."

But I paused.

In this case, I knew from various NFL sources that Brown was very interested in Garrett.

Yes, the Browns needed a quarterback. Yes, Mentor High School product Trubisky suddenly had become the hot name in that draft despite starting only 13 games at North Carolina. That was as a junior. He had been a backup his first two seasons.

I knew Sashi Brown well enough to understand how his analytics driven front office viewed the draft. The most valuable commodity was a quarterback—the right quarterback. No mathematical equations are needed to figure that out. Number two on their list was a pass rusher.

Former Browns CEO Joe Banner, although no longer with the team in 2017, explained the analytic approach this way: "The most important guy is the quarterback and a good passing game. Then comes rushing the quarterback and stopping the opponent's passing game."

I believe the Browns floated some rumors about their interest in Trubisky because that's what teams do as the draft approaches.

As for Garrett, here's what Steve Palazzolo of Pro Football Focus wrote at the time:

> If Michelangelo were sculpting the perfect edge rusher, he'd likely come up with something similar to Garrett. Throw every scouty term in the book Garrett's way and he resembles it—burst, bend, twitchy, you name it—but most importantly, Garrett is not just an athletic projection for the next level. He's used all of his tools to produce on the field, and he's done so at a dominant level for three years.

I knew the Browns agreed with that opinion. A few weeks before the draft, I wrote:

I think it's Garrett. I want it to be Garrett. It makes sense in a draft with seemingly no big-time quarterbacks for it to be Garrett. The defensive end is supposed to be the best pass rusher in the draft. As the analytics people study the trends in salaries, the highest-paid position is quarterback. No surprise there. But No. 2 is pass rushers such as Von Miller. By taking Garrett, the Browns will have him under control for five seasons at reasonable dollars. That assumes he does become a Pro Bowl player.

* * *

The Browns never admitted they had second thoughts about how they worked "The Plan" in 2016. But they did. The 1-15 record in 2016 did lead to the No. 1 pick in the 2017 draft. But the next season would be even worse, leading to a short-term public relations disaster with the fans.

The Browns entered the 2017 draft with a pair of first rounders (No. 1 and No. 12) and their eyes focused on Myles Garrett as the top pick.

The Browns still needed a quarterback. The guys who had played the position for the Browns in 2016 were Josh McCown, Robert Griffin III and Cody Kessler. McCown and Griffin were free agents and headed elsewhere.

When it came time for the Browns to use that No. 12 pick, Houston was on the phone. The Texans wanted the selection to draft Deshaun Watson. The Browns were still looking to accumulate more draft picks.

They traded the No. 12 pick to Houston—who indeed selected Watson, the star quarterback from Clemson—for the No. 25 pick plus Houston's first-round pick in 2018.

The Browns also traded up with Green Bay to add the No. 29 pick in the 2017 draft. They came away with three first-round selections: Garrett, safety Jabrill Peppers and tight end David Njoku.

That was a productive first round. Garrett has been one of the

It's hard to believe the Browns could have done any better in the 2017 draft than Myles Garrett. But . . . *Joshua Gunter / cleveland.com*

NFL's top defensive players. Njoku made a Pro Bowl as a tight end. Peppers started for two years at safety and then in 2019 was traded to the Giants in the Odell Beckham Jr. deal.

But the Browns still needed a quarterback. In the second round, they took Notre Dame's DeShone Kizer. He started 25 games at Notre Dame, throwing 47 touchdown passes compared to 19 interceptions. His Irish coach was Brian Kelly, who publicly said Kizer should have stayed in school.

Some scouting reports on Kizer . . .

Sports Illustrated's Chris Burke wrote:

> When it all clicks for Kizer . . . hoo boy. He is a prototypical NFL quarterback prospect (6-foot-4, 233 pounds) with quick, active feet, the athleticism to hurt defenses on the ground and the arm to zip the ball into tight windows. As Notre Dame's QB, he really challenged defenses in the window between the second and third levels—some of his best throws, consistently, were up the seam into that gap. He can get it deep and outside the numbers, too, with enough touch to drop those passes into a bucket. His player comp here, to Big Ben [Roethlisberger], mainly has to do with his size and passing acumen. Like the Steelers' QB, Kizer can look over the top of defenses and freeze safeties with a lethal pump fake before coming back to an open receiver. He keeps his feet moving, too, both inside the pocket and out of it, so that he can throw on the run . . . The team that drafts him will be taking a leap of faith.

NFL.com's Lance Zierlein:

> Kizer has the size and arm strength that should make him an early first-round pick, but his inconsistent accuracy and field vision could lead him to fall further than some expect.

ESPN's Mel Kiper:

> The Notre Dame underclassman who, like Mahomes, is raw and talented. His college coach made news by saying Kizer should have stayed in school for another year, and I have said that all along. He needs a year or two behind a veteran in the NFL . . .

Unfortunately for Kizer, he was picked by the Browns.

Coach Hue Jackson put Kizer into the 2017 starting lineup. He played 15 games, losing them all. He threw 22 interceptions (most in the NFL that season) and had only 11 touchdown passes. He was on an awful team and put in a hopeless situation. Kizer never started another NFL game. He was with the Packers for a while in 2018. He bounced around practice squads with several different teams in the next few years.

* * *

Given the fact that seven-time Super Bowl champion Tom Brady was a sixth-round pick in 1999, teams missing on Mahomes should not be a total surprise. At least he was a first-round pick.

But remember this, no one—and I mean no one—projected Mahomes to be one of the best NFL quarterbacks—ever. Many draft analysts at the time didn't even believe he deserved to be picked in the first round.

ESPN's Mel Kiper gave Kansas City a C+ for its draft:

> This class will hinge on Patrick Mahomes because Kansas City bet big that he's the successor to Alex Smith. Giving up a third-round pick and next year's first to move up 17 spots was a ton for a team with immediate needs elsewhere and some defenders getting up there in age. Mahomes has a high ceiling, but he's going to have to learn how NFL offenses are run, and the Chiefs are going to have to rebuild his mechanics from the ground up. Andy Reid and John Dorsey know what they're getting (and know what they're doing) and see some Brett Favre in Mahomes. And they have a capable quarterback in Alex Smith signed until 2019. This is a pick—and grade—that could look great or silly in five or six years.

For USA Today and other publications, Steven Ruiz wrote:

> Calling Mahomes a project is a major understatement. He's nowhere near ready to play in the NFL. And, honestly, he may never be. Between his inconsistent accuracy due to poor mechanics, his tendency to bail from clean pockets and his lack of

> field vision, he's going to leave as many big plays on the field as he creates. This was a risky pick.

Draft expert Dane Brugler on Mahomes:

> He's a complete projection because he's playing backyard football out there. Not much structure. It's easy to say, 'Well, give him a year or two in development and you'll have something.' Except that a lot of it is muscle memory. He's used to playing quarterback his way. It's not easy to take him out of what he's always done and turn him into something else. So the second-round range is where I would take a chance on Mahomes, but he's probably going to go in the first round somewhere. It's earlier than I would take him, but I understand why a team might pull the trigger that early, because he has the arm talent, the size, the mobility that you want.

Just like with Brady, no one saw Mahomes coming. Most teams apparently didn't have a first-round grade on him. Interesting question: If Mahomes, like Kizer, had been drafted by the Browns and forced to play right away on a bad team, how would he be viewed now? Would he have become another quarterback ruined by the Browns?

Mahomes went to Kansas City, a team with a 12-4 record in 2016. He sat behind veteran Alex Smith in 2017, starting only one game. It wasn't until 2018 that the Chiefs handed the offense to Mahomes. That never would have happened in Cleveland.

Finally, what about Mitch Trubisky, the player many experts projected the Browns would take . . . The player picked ahead of Mahomes and Watson? He was a so-so starter in his first four NFL seasons with Chicago, then became a backup with Buffalo and Pittsburgh.

THE HYPE MACHINE AND ODELL BECKHAM JR.

The cover of the 2019 Sports Illustrated NFL preview edition had this headline:

> THE BROWNS ARE BACK.
> Bold Prediction! Cleveland's first division title in 30 years.
> Can they win Super Bowl LIV?
> Turn to page 58.

Inside, Ben Baskin's story on the Browns ran under this headline: "Welcome to Cleveland Where the Browns Are True Contenders."

Early in the story, Baskin writes: "Thanks to some bold moves and brash personalities, the league's biggest losers of the last two decades—yes, the Cleveland Browns—are Super Bowl contenders."

There was more . . .

> In the 20 seasons since the Browns were reestablished as an expansion franchise, they have been the least successful, most dysfunctional organization in the NFL: a .298 winning percentage, nine general managers, 11 coaches," wrote Baskin in that 2019 preview. "Just 18 months ago they were capping off the

> worst three-season stretch ever. But something unimaginable was building in the background of that pain. Years of concerted demolition followed by a complete and rapid rebuild, a confluence of events both savvily plotted and serendipitously stumbled upon, led to this unforeseeable reality: The Browns enter 2019 with the sixth-best odds to win Super Bowl LIV. This team has not only talent in abundance but also an identity that reflects its city, with a cast-off, nose-to-the-grindstone GM; a long-toiling, nothing-came-easy coach; an undersized QB, constantly circling (or inventing) slights; and two exiled receivers, each looking to reshape his narrative.

This is not to knock Baskin. In 2019, the national media was in love with the Browns, desperately wanting them to be a classic football feel-good story. Baskin was riding the wave that began when Odell came to town.

That's Odell as in Odell Beckham Jr., acquired by the Browns in a trade with the New York Giants.

Most of us in the media just called him OBJ—easier to write in our stories.

The hype machine was steaming from the moment the March 13, 2019 trade was announced. It was one hot take after another about how the Browns were now contenders thanks to OBJ. He was big time in New York. More than a football player—he was a celebrity. He had been on the cover of GQ Magazine. He went to New York's Met Gala fashion event. He vacationed in Paris. He loved fashion. Yes, he was from Louisiana, but after being drafted by the Giants, he quickly became a New York kind of guy.

The capital of the national media certainly is not Parma or Garfield Heights. OBJ loved New York and the bright lights of Broadway. He savored every bite he took out of the Big Apple's night life.

Now, he was headed to Cleveland . . . and not happy about it.

As he told Sports Illustrated in that preseason story: "This [the

Browns fans couldn't wait to see Odell Beckham Jr. bring his talent to Cleveland. He wasn't as enthusiastic about the move. *Joshua Gunter / cleveland.com*

trade] was no business move. This was personal. They thought they'd send me here to die."

That should have been a warning sign to the Browns, but they viewed it another way. They thought it would fuel OBJ to excel and prove the Giants wrong.

Not quite.

* * *

Trading for OBJ was the second big swing taken by the Browns since their return in 1999. A gamble, a massive move that also drew national attention to the Browns. The first was drafting Johnny Manziel in 2014. This decision, though, was far riskier.

First, some context. In the 2016 and 2017 seasons, the Browns were 1-31. If you want to roll it back another year, from 2015 to 2017 the record was 4-44.

In 2018, Browns GM John Dorsey watched the team finish the

season at 7-8-1. They went 5-3 after interim head coach Gregg Williams took over for Hue Jackson (2-5-1 record). Quarterback Baker Mayfield looked worthy of his No. 1 draft position. Nick Chubb was emerging as an elite NFL running back. Myles Garrett was maturing into one of the NFL's premier pass rushers. Jarvis Landry was a very good possession receiver.

Now, Dorsey wanted to make a major move, one that would push the Browns into the playoffs—for several seasons.

Dorsey wanted a game-changing receiver. He had been in love with OBJ for a few years. And Dorsey was close to Giants GM David Gettleman.

Their deal was. . .

To Cleveland: OBJ.

To New York: Safety Jabrill Peppers plus the No. 17 and 95 picks in the 2019 draft.

The deal received an "A" from ESPN's Bill Barnwell, who wrote:

> Months after paying him a $20 million signing bonus, they traded one of the league's best young players at any position to the Browns for the sort of offer the computer would reject in a video game. This has the potential to be a franchise-resetting trade, the sort of deal that gets everyone fired and leaves fans muttering for decades about what could have been. The Giants have never had a player like OBJ before. Now, they don't have him — or much of anything — at all.

Actually, this was the second of two deals. A few days earlier, the Browns traded guard Kevin Zeitler to New York for defensive end Olivier Vernon. The two teams continued to talk. That led to the focus on OBJ as Dorsey became even more desperate to bring him to Cleveland. Most of the reviews suggested that the Browns had fleeced the Giants. OBJ would help the Browns fly high.

Many fans in Cleveland were excited about the trade.

I was lukewarm. One of my stories ran under this headline: "Why Did the Giants Want to Trade OBJ?"

New York dealt OBJ nine months after signing him to a five-year, $90 million ($65 million guaranteed) contract extension. My concern was partly the drama that comes with OBJ, one of the NFL's classic diva receivers. But a bigger issue was his injury history: He had played only 16 of 32 games in the previous two seasons.

The Browns didn't seem to care about his injury history.

"He's probably one of the two best receivers in the National Football League," Dorsey said at the time of the deal. "Very rarely do you get a chance to acquire a player of this magnitude. He's at a relatively young age. He's got a lot of football left in him. Great hands, great work ethic, committed, competitive, he really wants to be great. And that's all you can ask for."

Beckham was only 26 when the trade was made. But I heard people in the know say "his body is older." He had major ankle surgery in 2017. He dealt with hamstring problems for years. He also battled with New York quarterback Eli Manning and others about not being a focal point of the offense—in his opinion.

I believe the Giants had second thoughts about signing OBJ to that major contract extension, partly because he was turning into an injury-prone receiver. Did they sign him to appease the fans, and then realize it was a bad idea?

"Some have questioned why we signed Odell and then traded him," Gettleman said during a press conference at the time of the deal. "We didn't sign him to trade him but obviously things changed. Frankly, what changed is that another team made an offer we couldn't refuse. As it turned out, the fact he was signed for five more years made him very attractive and allowed us to get legitimate value."

Gettleman and the Giants were being ripped in New York. He kept explaining the trade:

"The obvious question is . . . why? After much discussion, we just believe this is in the best interests of the New York football Giants. I want everybody to know this was purely a football business decision. There's no intrigue, there's no he-said, she-said, none of that stuff. Odell is a tremendous talent, which made him a valuable asset. With football being the ultimate team game, we turned that fact into three valuable assets, at the very least."

* * *

Jim Brown was quoted in the Sports Illustrated story as saying, "It seems Jesus has been at work. It seems almost like Cleveland is back on top, like it should be."

During training camp, Browns fans were chanting "Super . . . BOWL . . . Super . . . BOWL."

The Browns entered the 2019 season with the sixth-best odds to win the Super Bowl. Even the odds-makers were sipping some of the giddy juice, apparently believing that new head coach Freddie Kitchens would be turned into the second-coming of Paul Brown or Marty Schottenheimer.

The Browns had been looking for a new head coach.

In the Browns Sports Illustrated preview, Baskin wrote:

> Entering the winter in search of a new coach, Dorsey put together a committee to find a 'leader of men' and whittled an initial list of 20-plus candidates to eight . . . After two months of looking, the committee came to what Dorsey says was a unanimous decision.

I have some doubts about the "unanimous decision" part.

On that search committee were Browns chief strategy officer Paul DePodesta and Andrew Berry, then an assistant Browns GM. Their candidate was Kevin Stefanski (who would become the Browns coach a year later). Dorsey had become enamored with Kitchens, whose playcalling as Browns offensive coordinator in

“Very rarely do you get a chance to acquire a player of this magnitude,” Browns GM John Dorsey said. But did the Browns pause to consider why the Giants were dealing the star receiver so soon after re-signing him to a big contract? *Joshua Gunter / cleveland.com*

2018 had helped Baker Mayfield thrive. Dorsey believed Kitchens and Mayfield were a magic combination. He didn’t want to risk losing Kitchens if he chose someone else for head coach—even though no other teams seemed interested in hiring him for that job.

At this point, Dorsey was the King of Cleveland, at least as far as Browns fans were concerned. His 2018 draft had delivered Baker Mayfield, Denzel Ward and Nick Chubb. His trade before the 2018 season for Jarvis Landry was a great move. Then came the OBJ deal, loved (at first) by nearly everyone.

Before the decision to hire Kitchens was made, I wrote this:

> Over the weekend, I had an NFL executive tell me the following: “If the Browns stay inside for a coach, it’s Freddie.” He meant Browns offensive coordinator Freddie Kitchens. “If the

Browns go outside, it's Campbell." The executive meant New Orleans associate head coach Dan Campbell.

I had written a column about how the Browns should seriously consider Campbell. He eventually would become the head coach of the Detroit Lions and lead their revival.

Campbell never had a chance. Neither did Stefanski or anyone else. If Dorsey wanted Kitchens as the head coach, ownership was willing to give him Kitchens.

At the press conference announcing his hiring, Kitchens made this comment: "I heard the other day somebody say I wasn't ready to be a head coach . . . I mean, who the hell is ready to be a head coach?"

It's a fair question when it comes to rookie head coaches. When it came to Kitchens, it didn't take long to see he wasn't ready for the strong personalities on the team combined with the pressure of coaching a Browns team with such great expectations.

* * *

Finally, it was time to play football. The Browns opened the 2019 season at home versus Tennessee, a solid team coached by Mike Vrabel that had had a 9-7 record in 2018. Vrabel, a Northeast Ohio native who played at Walsh Jesuit High School and Ohio State, used the hype around the Browns to inspire his team.

Browns fans packed the stands. As the 1 p.m. kickoff approached, they were woofing about a Super Bowl and dreaming about Mayfield saving the franchise.

During the game, OBJ wore a watch—a $190,000 Richard Mille watch. He explained that he wore it during practice, too, and even showered with it on.

Oh, boy.

A little more than three hours later, the Browns had been flagged for 18 penalties. That's right, 18 penalties. No Browns team since 1999—yes, the first year of expansion—had ever been penalized 18 times.

Those penalties cost them 182 yards in a 43-13 loss.

Kitchens, who sometimes had his players run laps after committing penalties, often said, "We don't practice penalties in training camp."

Apparently, they were saving that for the regular season games.

The Browns also had two players ejected from that first game for fighting, including kicking an opponent in the head. Mayfield was picked off three times. He was sacked five times.

The game was a jarring preview for what was to come in that 2019 season.

The Browns finished the season at 6-10. But at least they did beat Pittsburgh. Although that was the game where Myles Garrett hit Pittsburgh quarterback Mason Rudolph in the head with a helmet. Rudolph did seem to kick Garrett in the groin area right before that, but however you score the fight, it was a mess. Garrett was suspended for the remaining six games of the season.

Despite winning 21-7, "It feels like we lost," Mayfield said after the game.

The Browns played the Steelers later in the season. A few days before the game, Kitchens wore a shirt reading "Pittsburgh Started It!"

The front office was furious with the rookie head coach. They wanted to back away from any more talk about the first Steelers game and the fight. Instead, the coach was a human billboard stirring up emotions the Browns wanted cooled off.

In the rematch, in Pittsburgh, the Browns lost 20-13. The Steelers beat Cleveland with their No. 3 quarterback, Devlin "The Duck" Hodges. The Browns left starting safety Damarious Randall back in Cleveland due to a "coach's decision"—he was being disciplined for something.

Kitchens never was able to keep the team under control.

Beckham played all 16 games. He rarely practiced during the week because he was dealing with cranky hamstrings. He dropped more passes (seven) than he had touchdown catches (four). He had a decent season with 74 receptions, but there were times when he was upset with Mayfield. Beckham believed he was open and Mayfield didn't see him—or choose to throw him the ball.

The team that was supposed to be a Super Bowl contender lost four of their last five games to finish at 6-10.

"No one said I was a finished product," Kitchens said following his final game as Browns coach.

No kidding.

Kitchens was fired. So was Dorsey. There were whispers that OBJ's camp had asked the Browns to trade the receiver.

* * *

Following the 2019 season, OBJ would play only 13 more games for the Browns.

In 2020, Kevin Stefanski replaced Kitchens as head coach. Stefanski brought order to the team and a more structured offense.

OBJ suffered a season-ending knee injury in the seventh game of the season. The offense was better without him. Too often, Mayfield had seemed focused on OBJ, trying to get the ball to him.

OBJ had only 23 catches in seven games before knee surgery ended his 2020 season. The Browns finished 11-5 and made the playoffs.

In 2021, OBJ was back. So was the question "Why doesn't OBJ get the ball more?" The answer was that OBJ's own performance had declined from his New York Pro Bowl days. He wasn't as fast. He had problems staying healthy.

He wanted out of Cleveland.

In six games with the Browns in 2021, OBJ caught only 17 passes. A video was posted on social media, allegedly by his father, titled

"Odell Beckham Is Always Open." It showed clips of Mayfield, during four games in the 2021 season, either making poor throws in OBJ's direction or not seeing him at all.

The Browns placed OBJ on waivers, and he was claimed by the Rams. He had some nice moments in L.A. His season ended with another knee injury—this one on Feb. 2, 2022, in the 2021 Super Bowl. That required another ACL surgery on the same knee as was operated on in 2020.

* * *

Both GMs who made the OBJ deal were soon gone. Dorsey was dispatched nine months after the deal—at the end of the 2019 season. New York GM Dave Gettleman retired after the 2021 season. He had a 19-46 record with the Giants.

Here is what the Giants received in the deal:

1. A first-round pick by the Browns in 2017, Jabrill Peppers went to New York and started 30 games in three seasons with the Giants. His next stop was New England. He had started 26 games there through 2024.

2. The Giants used the No. 95 pick on Oshane Ximines, who became a part-time player as a linebacker/defensive end.

3. Then there's Dexter Lawrence. With the No. 17 pick in the 2019 draft from Cleveland, the Giants selected the 6-foot-4, 340-pound nose tackle from Clemson. He made Pro Bowls in 2022, 2023 and 2024. In 2023, he signed a four-year, $90 million extension with the Giants.

After leaving the Browns in the middle of the 2021 season, OBJ played 31 games, catching 71 passes (eight TDs) for three different teams—the Rams, Baltimore and Miami. He was released by the Dolphins in the middle of the 2024 season. Injuries continued to be a problem for him.

What do the Browns have to show for the OBJ deal? Nothing.

* * *

FANS WRITE IN ABOUT OBJ . . .

About Odell Beckham Jr., I don't blame them for trying. It sounded good, looked good. I believe it was a mix of we failed him and he failed us. I don't believe the team was in a place to have that kind of personality come in.

— Dan Funk, Aurora, Indiana

When we got OBJ, I cried tears of joy. He was such a dynamic talent and I thought it would lead us to Super Bowls. When I saw the on-field product, I just thought he was never utilized correctly and I truly believe the media and fans pushed a narrative that he was difficult. I saw a man who wanted to win, and people demonized him for it.

— Thomas Roth, Ashtabula, Ohio

Thinking about Odell Beckham, I have the same feeling almost as the Watson trade. Bring in a problem and it'll be a problem.

— Tom Yochim, Erie, Pennsylvania

Anyone who buys a Rolls and puts a little image of themselves as the hood ornament—I got ZERO time for that nonsense. Then the thing with his father. I was happy to see the back of him leaving town. I guess the players really liked him but to me he broke the cardinal rule of football: NO ONE is bigger than the team.

— Mark Friedlander, Shaker Heights, Ohio

HERE WE GO AGAIN: GREAT EXPECTATIONS

I can close my eyes and see the picture. There's Baker Mayfield and Myles Garrett leaping in utter unimaginable joy. Mayfield is hugging a football. Garrett is laughing. The two men jump up at the same time and touch shoulders in midair.

That's what happened when the Browns beat the Steelers in the playoffs after the 2020 season.

Didn't it seem like the start of something big, something special?

Both were 25 years old. Garrett was the No. 1 pick in the 2017 draft. Mayfield was the No. 1 pick in the 2018 draft. A passer and a pass rusher leading the Browns to the playoffs for the first time in 17 years.

It was Jan. 10, 2021. The world was still in the grim fist of the COVID-19 pandemic. The game was played in a nearly empty Heinz Field in Pittsburgh because of NFL safety protocols. That fall and winter, the Browns were bringing some hope and light into the darkness that seemed to hang over everything.

Here's part of what I wrote that night from Pittsburgh:

> I never thought I'd write a story like this.
>
> Not about the Browns. Not about the Browns playing like they did Sunday in Pittsburgh against the Steelers in the playoffs.

Not about the Browns scoring 35 points in the first half. Not about the Steelers turning the ball over four times. Not the Browns out-coaching the Steelers when their head coach was watching from his basement.

You can't make this up. Usually when I write that phrase, something unbelievably abominable has happened to the Browns.

Not this: Browns 48, Pittsburgh 37.

But yes, that was the final score. Let's repeat it: Browns 48, Pittsburgh 37.

Say it out loud: Browns 48, Pittsburgh 37.

The Browns hadn't won at Heinz Field since 2003, a 17-game losing streak. Browns fans are on a first-name basis with all the ghosts of Browns late-game collapses on this field.

And these are the Steelers. As painful as it is to admit, they are one of the NFL's most consistent and elite franchises. They weren't about to just quit against the Browns.

And they didn't, but the Browns won, anyway.

That's right, they beat the same Ben Roethlisberger who took a 24-2-1 career record versus the Browns into the game. He threw *four* interceptions.

This wasn't a win, it was a WOW!"

* * *

The Browns went from a chaotic 6-10 season under Freddie Kitchens to 11-5 with new Coach Kevin Stefanski and GM Andrew Berry in charge. Mayfield adapted to Stefanski's offense featuring a lot of play-action passes and generally smart football.

Mayfield threw 26 touchdown passes compared to eight interceptions. He completed 63% of his passes. It was the best season by any Browns quarterback since the team returned in 1999.

I remember thinking, *It looks like the Browns got this right.*

It didn't mean a Super Bowl. But how about a team that stacks up a few winning seasons and playoff appearances? How about a GM/coach combination that works together and makes sound decisions? How about a team that was becoming like the team they just defeated—the Steelers?

That 11-5 record in 2020 didn't appear to be a fluke.

The Browns had one of those in 2007. That was when Derek Anderson, seemingly out of nowhere (the Baltimore Ravens' practice squad), led the Browns to a 10-6 record. Even during the 2007 season, there was a sense Anderson would fade. He had a strong arm, but was not an accurate passer. He wasn't mobile. Nor did he come across as confident.

That was a Halley's Comet season. It came, then disappeared. Anderson would make only 31 starts in the rest of his career: a 10-21 record, throwing more interceptions (37) than touchdown passes (26). In some ways, he still had a remarkable career for a sixth-rounder in 2005 with little optimism predicted for a pro career. He'd play 11 more years after 2007, nearly all of it as a backup.

Baker Mayfield was different.

Mayfield was the No. 1 draft choice. His 2020 season was his second good performance in three years. As a rookie in 2018, his 27 touchdown passes were an NFL rookie record. He threw for 3,725 yards—sixth most in Browns history. He had a 6-7 record as a starter. The team was 0-16 in the prior season.

Look at the exciting rookie season (2018), the struggling sophomore season (2019) and then the strong comeback season (2020). It is easy to write off 2019 as part of a generally messy season.

After beating Pittsburgh in the first round of the playoffs, the Browns traveled to Kansas City for the next round. They lost 22-17 to a Chiefs team that eventually won the Super Bowl.

Here's part of my story after the loss in Kansas City:

> The Browns were one of the best stories in football, going from the chaos of 6-10 to an 11-5 record under Stefanski in his

rookie season. Mayfield proved he can be a QB who can take his team into the playoffs and beat Pittsburgh in back-to-back games.

I loved this season. I loved the character shown by the team. I loved how they stayed away from drama and the needless dumb things the Browns have done in the past.

Disappointed by the loss in KC?

Absolutely.

But right now, I can't wait for next year as the Andrew Berry front office has the offseason to bolster the defense.

* * *

At the start of the 2021 Browns season, Stefanski was the 2020 NFL Coach of the Year. He was considered a quarterback whisperer, an elite teacher for how he pulled Mayfield out of his 2019 malaise and turned him into one of the NFL's top 10 ranked quarterbacks.

GM Andrew Berry had added veterans through trades and free agent signings to help the defense.

ESPN's Jake Trotter wrote:

> Cleveland's defense will be among the league's most improved. With eight new defensive starters, the Browns might struggle defensively for the first month or so of the season. But down the stretch, Cleveland will boast one of the five best defenses in the league, elevating the Browns into a legitimate Super Bowl contender.

There is it again, the dreaded two words in a Browns prediction: Super Bowl.

There was more.

NFL.com's Jeffri Chadiha wrote:

> The Cleveland Browns have built one of the best rosters in football. They used the draft and free agency to load up on ath-

> letic players to improve a mediocre defense, while quarterback Baker Mayfield has learned to maximize all the talent around him on offense . . . The Browns look to be the biggest threat to the Kansas City Chiefs for AFC supremacy.

Sports Illustrated's Conor Orr wrote a story under this headline: "Why the Browns are poised to knock off Pittsburgh and Baltimore in the AFC's tightest three-team race."

Alex Ballentine of Bleacher Report wrote:

> The front office has done everything it can to fix the remaining holes from last year's team. Bringing in Troy Hill and John Johnson III gives them veteran help to fix the secondary, while drafting Greg Newsome II and Jeremiah Owusu-Koramoah gives them two potential Rookie of the Year contenders.
>
> Signing Jadeveon Clowney provides them with an additional threat up front. He isn't the pass-rusher he used to be, but he's an elite run defender. That's all paired with the aforementioned offense with all the tools to be elite. Winning games in a variety of ways is key to success in the playoffs. The Browns are built to do just that. They have the run game and defense to win ugly and the pass-catching talent with an emergent quarterback in Baker Mayfield to win in a shootout.
>
> An AFC Championship game against Kansas City is a coin toss, but the Browns have everything in place to play for a conference title.

Then there was me.

I was no better . . . or worse . . . than the rest. Here's part of my preview column for the 2021 season:

> Since Kevin Stefanski took over as coach, the growth Mayfield has shown on the field and in his public statements is remarkable.

Is he a great QB? Too early to go that far. But he's good. He's durable. He led the team to the playoffs last season and he'll do it again in 2021. The Browns have a maturing QB in his fourth pro season working in an offense that accentuates his strengths. They also have a coaching staff that doesn't panic, which wasn't the case earlier in Mayfield's career.

Know why you should feel good about the Browns? Because what the front office and coaching staff do what makes sense. It won't always work out, but there is reason to believe these guys will figure things out when adversity hits.

I pick them to finish 11-6, make the playoffs and reach the AFC title game.

* * *

These Browns were supposed to be "Tough, Smart and Accountable." That's the gospel Stefanski and Berry were preaching almost from the moment they arrived to work together in Cleveland.

Before the 2020 season, I had a long interview with Berry.

"Discipline and being tough, smart, accountable are interrelated," said Berry. "It stems from a common vision. It's what we want organizationally: Kevin [Stefanski], Paul [DePodesta] and myself. Those three traits will enable us to have a good team."

I liked that approach. For too many years, the Browns were none of those things—or at least some of them but with one attribute missing. In 2019, the Browns were undisciplined and disorganized. Over the years, every team had some players who were tough . . . some players who were smart . . . some players who were accountable. But they never had enough.

Nor did most of the front office and coaching staff publicly talk about those values and then push the team to follow the mantra.

"I want our team to be disciplined and resilient every week," said Berry. "I want us to be prepared to deal with the inevitable adversity in a strong, positive fashion."

Cleveland Browns executive vice president and GM Andrew Berry (left) and head coach Kevin Stefanski wanted players who were "Tough, Smart and Accountable." They got just enough of them in 2020 to reach the playoffs.
John Kuntz / cleveland.com

The Browns opened the 2020 season being spanked 38-6 in Baltimore. *Same old Browns,* had to run through most of our minds. But then they beat Cincinnati, 35-30, the next week to begin a four-game winning streak.

Then they were crushed 38-7 in Pittsburgh. It was a demoralizing performance, or at least that could have been the case. But the Browns went 7-3 to finish the season at 11-5 and make the playoffs.

The 2020 Browns were something special. Nick Chubb, Denzel Ward, Jarvis Landry, Myles Garrett, Joel Bitonio, JC Tretter, Kareem Hunt and even role players such as Charley Hughlett, Rashard Higgins and Donovan Peoples-Jones were the heartbeat of a team that overachieved.

And there was Mayfield, showing he could indeed be a long-term quarterback for the Browns.

Before the Browns opened the 2021 season in Kansas City,

Chiefs Coach Andy Reid talked about Stefanski. They both have Philadelphia roots. Reid coached the Eagles before heading to K.C. Stefanski played at St. Joseph's Prep in Philadelphia.

"He's thorough and dedicated to the game," said Reid. "He's a smart kid. You can see it in his (football) operation."

It was most apparent when Stefanski and some of his assistants couldn't coach the playoff game in Pittsburgh while being quarantined due to COVID-19 protocol restrictions, but the Browns still won, 48-37.

That Browns victory in Pittsburgh was a perfect example of Tough, Smart and Accountable. Stefanski was in the basement of his suburban Cleveland home while Offensive Coordinator Alex Van Pelt called the plays.

If you're a Browns fan, you should have been proud of that tough, smart and accountable team.

There were reasons to expect more of that in 2021.

HOW IT ALL FELL APART: BAKER AND OBJ

You might be surprised to know that Odell Beckham Jr. attended Baker Mayfield's wedding. That was in the summer of 2019. Mayfield and OBJ often played video games together and were friends, at least for the first two years (2019–20) of their time in Cleveland. Along with a few other teammates, they took a short vacation together in Big Sky, Montana, during Labor Day before the 2021 season began.

Off the field, Mayfield and OBJ connected. OBJ liked to do that with his teammates, going back to his days with the New York Giants. He sometimes bought new shoes for teammates—and also for equipment room staff and trainers. OBJ loved to collect shoes and clothes. He'd open his closets at home to teammates, especially rookies or those on non-guaranteed contracts.

Some of these details came from Jake Trotter, an excellent reporter for ESPN. Trotter also has a close relationship with Mayfield, having covered him when he played for the University of Oklahoma. Along with cleveland.com's Mary Kay Cabot, Trotter did some of the best reporting on the OBJ/Mayfield relationship as it disintegrated.

As the 2021 season approached, both OBJ and Mayfield were

anxious. Mayfield thought he was in line for a lucrative contract extension. He was three years into the four-year rookie contract he had signed in 2018. Quarterbacks who have good years in their first three NFL seasons often receive a contract extension. Mayfield believed he had earned one. He had a strong 2018 rookie season. Yes, the 2019 season was a mess, but much of that had to do with coach Freddie Kitchens and the overall lack of structure the team needed during a 6-10 season. In 2020, he bounced back, ranking in the NFL's top 10 quarterbacks according to various rating services.

Here was Mayfield's contract situation as the 2021 season approached:

2021 salary, $10 million.

2022 team option, $18.8 million.

In April 2021, the Browns picked up Mayfield's team option for 2022. Media covering the Browns assumed the Browns would use that as the base for a long-term lucrative extension. But the Browns never had a serious contract extension discussion with Mayfield. This bothered Mayfield. He thought he deserved it after leading the Browns to their first playoff victory since the franchise returned in 1999.

* * *

Now it's worth looking at Mayfield's background. He was a star at Lake Travis High School in Austin, Texas. He wanted to play for Oklahoma or another big-time college program. Despite his superb high school career, he was rated a 3-star recruit (out of a possible five stars) by ESPN. A story on the website stated: "Mayfield appears to be poised, tough and under control. We are not sure any of Mayfield's traits are elite or unique. He is sound with redeeming qualities, but is also a guy that will receive mostly non-BCS conference level attention."

His scholarship offers came from New Mexico, Florida Atlantic, Rice and Washington State. Why the reluctance from major programs? Mayfield is only 6-foot. He doesn't appear to be especially athletic. Mayfield decided to find a higher rated program that would take him as a non-scholarship walk-on. That program was Texas Tech. There, Mayfield surprised the coaching staff by winning the starting job as a freshman.

Mayfield was voted the Big 12 "Freshman Offensive Player of the Year," but he had an up-and-down season as he battled some injuries while playing eight games. By the end of the season, Texas Tech head coach Kliff Kingsbury met with Mayfield, who still wasn't on a football scholarship. Mayfield contends Kingsbury never offered a scholarship for his sophomore year until Mayfield left for home and was thinking of transferring. Klingsbury disputed that report. But the real problem was the coach would not guarantee a starting spot to Mayfield. Texas Tech had a much higher rated recruit named Davis Webb (who later played a bit in the NFL).

Mayfield had gone to Texas Tech as a fallback from his dream school—Oklahoma. Now, he decided to leave Texas Tech and transfer to Oklahoma, even if it meant trying out for the team as a walk-on. Oklahoma head coach Lincoln Riley was aware of Mayfield and welcomed him. But Mayfield first had to earn a scholarship. That didn't take long. Mayfield started three years. He eventually became the top pick in the 2018 NFL draft by the Browns.

Why this brief history lesson?

Because Mayfield was resentful about his lack of recruitment from the top college programs when he was coming out of high school. He felt disrespected by Texas Tech, which didn't immediately offer him a scholarship after he won the starting quarterback job as a freshman.

Mayfield has always seen himself as the scrappy underdog, the guy who was too small . . . too slow . . . too something. He almost expected to be doubted because it had happened to him before.

Then he became the No. 1 pick in the NFL draft. That put him in the exalted class.

Except, the Browns were unwilling to make a major long-term commitment as the 2021 season approached. They picked up the team option of $18.8 million for 2022, but that was it.

While Mayfield never publicly said so, that bothered him. It became one of the underlying themes of the 2021 Browns season.

* * *

Odell Beckham Jr. comes from a family that was like athletic royalty at LSU. His mother, Heather Van Norman, was a track star at the school. She won several NCAA titles. His father, Odell Beckham Sr., was a running back for the Tigers—mostly a backup, appearing in 28 games over three seasons and rushing for 757 yards.

OBJ was a 4-star recruit as a receiver out of Isidore Newman High School in New Orleans. He was recruited by many major college programs but chose LSU, where he was a star. He became a first-round pick in the 2014 draft, selected at No. 12 by the New York Giants. The Browns had a chance to select him. They had the No. 8 pick, which they used on Justin Gilbert—a cornerback from Oklahoma State. That turned out to be a draft disaster for the Browns. Gilbert started three games in three NFL seasons.

OBJ became an instant star in New York. In his first three seasons, he made three Pro Bowls. He caught 288 passes, 35 for TDs. He embraced the glitter of New York City, attending fashion shows and quickly becoming a celebrity. OBJ was a gifted athlete, fast and agile. He was a highlight film of off-balance, one-handed catches.

From 2014 to 2016, OBJ averaged 96 catches per season.

Then came the injuries, most of them with his legs. In 2017 and 2018, he played only 16 of 32 games for the Giants.

Then came frustration. He feuded with coaches and quarterback Eli Manning about not being targeted with more passes.

Then he was traded to the Browns.

OBJ didn't want to leave New York. Cleveland didn't appeal to him.

The first time he asked to be traded by the Browns was after

OBJ (right) attended Baker Mayfield's wedding in 2019. But they struggled to connect on the field, and by 2021 Mayfield was taking heat for it. It didn't end well for the Browns. *Joshua Gunter / cleveland.com*

the 2019 season. In 2020, he played the first seven games for the Browns, catching 23 passes. He then suffered a season-ending knee injury Oct. 25. It required ACL surgery.

His 2019 and 2020 seasons showed few hints of the game-breaking OBJ of his early years.

While friends off the field, Baker Mayfield and OBJ struggled to connect during games. In those two seasons, many postgame Browns press conferences featured questions such as, "Why isn't OBJ getting the ball more?" That happened even after the team was winning in 2020. What no one with the Browns wanted to say publicly was that OBJ's speed and athleticism had declined from his New York days. The leg injuries were a factor.

OBJ was being paid $15.75 million by the Browns for 2021. He was also under contract in 2022—but not a dollar was guaranteed.

Like Mayfield, OBJ worried that the Browns weren't going to

give him a new long-term deal. He also believed that head coach Kevin Stefanski's offense didn't make the most of his skills. As for Mayfield, OBJ had doubts about the quarterback's ability. When you consider where the two players stood in terms of their own careers, what happened in 2021 isn't a shock.

General manager John Dorsey was gone, replaced by new GM Andrew Berry. It was Dorsey who traded for OBJ, and it was Dorsey who drafted Mayfield. Money often hangs over situations when things go wrong, as they did for OBJ and Mayfield in 2021.

* * *

The Browns opened the 2021 season in Kansas City, and they expected OBJ to play. He talked about being ready for the game. About two hours before kickoff, OBJ tested his surgically repaired knee, running barefoot on the field and catching a few passes. Then, he decided to sit out. The Browns were surprised, but didn't make an issue of it because OBJ was coming off major knee surgery.

The Browns lost to the Chiefs, 33-29. Mayfield was terrific, completing 21 of 28 passes for 321 yards and a touchdown. He completed passes to eight different players.

The next week, the Browns beat Houston, 31-21. OBJ still didn't play. Mayfield completed 19 of 21 passes for 213 yards. He threw for a touchdown, and also ran for one.

In his first two games, Mayfield had completed 82% of his passes. He seemed to be the same Baker Mayfield who ended the 2020 season as a top-10 rated NFL quarterback.

But in the second quarter of that victory over Houston, Mayfield threw an interception, and during the runback he tried to make a tackle. After the play, his left arm was bothering him. Mayfield left the game, but quickly returned, and finished the game. There were no indications that he had suffered a significant injury.

Later, though, it would be learned Mayfield had suffered a torn labrum in his left (non-throwing) shoulder. He started wearing a harness. The Browns kept saying the injury had no impact on his passing. Mayfield insisted he wanted to play. But something was very wrong with him. His accuracy was off.

Meanwhile, OBJ returned to the field. In his first game back—a 26-6 victory over Chicago—he caught five passes for 77 yards. But then he caught only two passes in each of his next two games.

When Mayfield was asked—over and over—"Why can't you get OBJ the ball more?", he said he wanted to do just that. But what Mayfield didn't say—and what was true—is that OBJ sometimes ran the wrong pass routes. It happens. (For example, on the interception that led to Mayfield's injury, receiver Anthony Schwartz was supposed to run one way but instead ran in the opposite direction.)

OBJ was known to "break off" the designated pass routes and run where he thought would lead to him being open. That created frustration for Mayfield. (As it did for other quarterbacks who threw to OBJ over the years.)

Mayfield's injury was also a factor. It was like the Browns and Mayfield were denying reality. At one point, I pressed a top Browns official about Mayfield's poor play and how it looked like he must really be hurt. The official pushed back, saying the left shoulder had nothing to do with Mayfield's sudden inaccurate passes. I said: "Look at the tape. He was one quarterback before the shoulder problem, a different one after. He's hurt."

During that nightmarish 2021 season, I wrote at least three columns begging the Browns to bench Mayfield in favor of backup Case Keenum. The Browns did sit Mayfield twice during the year—one game each time—but never sat him down for the several weeks that were needed.

* * *

OBJ had asked the Browns to trade him after the 2020 season. No way that would happen. He was still recovering from the ACL knee injury. He had little trade value. In his third game back in 2021, the Browns lost 47-42 to the Chargers in Los Angeles. Mayfield was terrific in that game. He looked healthy, completing 23 of 32 passes for 305 yards and a pair of TDs. This was the odd part of the 2021 season for Mayfield. Often, he looked hurt. But there were a few games when suddenly he played like the healthy Mayfield of 2020.

That game in L.A. was basically the end of OBJ with the Browns, although he would remain with the team for a few more weeks. OBJ has a lot of friends on the West Coast in the movie business. He invited several to the game. His parents were there. So were some NBA players, including LeBron James. Then, he caught just two passes for 20 yards. He was furious about being targeted only three times, especially with his friends at the game.

Once again, OBJ asked the Browns to trade him. No team was interested in him with his $15.7 million salary.

On Nov. 2, the OBJ camp posted to his father's Instagram account an 11-minute video purporting to demonstrate how Beckham was "always open" yet Mayfield didn't throw him the ball.

"Deliberately not throwing the ball to an extremely talented player that I've put a lot of work in with . . . it's an opinionated statement, I'll say that," Mayfield said at a press conference right after the video was released.

The Browns were now trying to trade OBJ. No one wanted him. They ended up releasing him Nov. 5. They even converted some of his salary into a signing bonus, to reduce the salary cap impact and make it easier for another team to pick him up on waivers. The Rams did, and signed OBJ.

* * *

OBJ and Mayfield never consistently connected on the field. According to ESPN, Mayfield had a QBR targeting rating of 58 (out of 100) when throwing to OBJ for the Browns. When throwing to any other Cleveland receiver, Mayfield's rating was 85.2.

After hurting his shoulder in 2021, Baker Mayfield took criticism for OBJ's on-field struggles. *John Kuntz / cleveland.com*

After hurting his shoulder in 2021, Mayfield took criticism for OBJ's on-field struggles, suggesting they resulted from Mayfield's inability to get him the ball. He was also being ripped by the media for his own inconsistent play. Mayfield became defensive in press conferences, sometimes questioning coach Kevin Stefanski's play calling.

Mayfield kept demanding to play. But when he played poorly, he wanted the media to cut him a break because he was hurt. This was noticed by some of Mayfield's teammates, who thought Mayfield was making excuses. They pointed out that several players besides Mayfield were battling injuries but they didn't use that as an explanation for their struggles. Some players backed OBJ, believing Mayfield was not working hard enough to get the ball to him. A smaller group supported Mayfield. The team was fracturing.

To be fair to Mayfield, no one with the Browns wanted to discuss the fact that OBJ didn't always run the proper pass patterns. The Browns also were in denial about Mayfield's injury.

Those who backed the Browns continuing to play Mayfield will mention how he completed 10 passes in a row after returning to the game against Houston—the game where the original injury occurred. That thinking was flawed because this is pro football. Quarterbacks take vicious hits in nearly every game. As the shoulder didn't heal, it became more painful over the course of the season. Mayfield also suffered a significant heel injury. At one point, it was said he had bruised ribs. I later heard at least one rib was broken. But the Browns kept playing him.

Mayfield's confidence was shaken. So was the Browns' faith in Mayfield. Before the end of the 2021 season, the Browns were already looking at other quarterback options for 2022.

I have never received a decent answer to the question of why the Browns continued to play Mayfield when he obviously was hurt. Browns coaches or front office staff would say, "He's medically cleared to play." I'd come back with, "Look how he's playing . . . if nothing else, he should be benched based on performance. Case Keenum is a respectable backup."

Some conspiracy theories suggest that the Browns continued to play Mayfield so he would "look bad." I guess that would make it easier for the Browns to go for another quarterback after the 2021 season. But that theory makes little sense. First, anyone working for Browns owner Jimmy Haslam knows he isn't afraid to fire people. From 2012 (when he bought the team) to the end of the 2021 season, Haslam fired five coaches and four GMs. Next, the team's record wasn't so awful that tanking for a high draft pick was an option.

The entire organization became paralyzed when it came to clearly evaluating Mayfield in 2021. The team was coming off the first playoff appearance (2020) in Haslam's ownership. There were great expectations for the season. It was as if they were hoping for a miracle with Mayfield and OBJ suddenly becoming a winning combination.

In some ways, OBJ and Mayfield destroyed each other in 2021. Both players were dealing with injuries. Both were frustrated with each other. Both sensed they were not in the Browns' long-term plans

* * *

As the 2021 season neared its end, the Browns became very serious about seeking a new quarterback to "take us to the next level," as I was told by a top official. They thought they could be good with Mayfield, but not great. Ownership was desperate to reach the Super Bowl. They turned their focus to Deshaun Watson, who had demanded a trade from Houston after sitting out the 2021 season.

After the 2021 season, Mayfield's camp was already indicating they'd be OK if the Browns traded him. This was before the Browns' pursuit of Watson became public.

On March 15, 2022, news broke of the Browns meeting with Watson. No deal was struck at that point. The next day, ESPN's Chris Mortensen reported Mayfield was done with the Browns, who, he was told, wanted "an adult" at quarterback. That remark outraged Mayfield. He posted a message on Twitter thanking Browns fans, but also asking to be traded.

On March 18, 2022, the Browns traded for Watson and signed him to a five-year, fully guaranteed $230 million contract.

It was at that time the largest guaranteed contract in NFL history.

In a meeting with the media, Jimmy Haslam said: "I know Baker felt that comment [about the Browns wanting 'an adult'] came from ownership, but that's not true. Baker gave it everything he had while he was here. Nobody can question his effort [in 2021] and nobody can question the four years he gave the city of Cleveland."

The late Chris Mortensen was a tremendous reporter, a man of integrity. If not Haslam, some high-ranking Browns official made that "adult" comment to him.

While Mayfield was waiting for the Browns to trade him, he went on a podcast called Ya Never Know. Mayfield didn't help himself with some comments—which also revealed his state of mind and frustrations during the 2021 season.

"It's a huge battle within the locker room in my position being a quarterback," Mayfield told the host. "Some of these guys don't play the game because they love it. They're playing it to get a retirement fund . . . They're making millions of dollars and they don't care about winning."

Perhaps Mayfield is right about that, but was this the time to call out your teammates? He was still with the Browns. Also, name names if you want to be a standup guy.

"How can I get the best out of people that are making a ton of money?" said Mayfield. "I could always motivate people when we weren't making money. . . . You get a pension after four years . . . how do you motivate people that are at that point?"

The interview was Mayfield at his most immature. Perhaps he said those things to push the Browns even harder to trade him. But he missed the point that teams interested in him would not be thrilled with those remarks.

Mayfield finally was traded to the Carolina Panthers. The Browns received in exchange a fifth-round pick in 2024. They also paid $10.5 million of Mayfield's $18.8 million salary. With that deal, the most successful Browns quarterback since the franchise returned in 1999 left town.

THE ODYSSEY OF DESHAUN WATSON

A "five-month odyssey" is what general manager Andrew Berry called the Browns' efforts to obtain Deshaun Watson when he introduced the team's new star quarterback to the Cleveland media and fans on March 25, 2022.

Actually, the saga begins long before the Browns even considered pursuing Watson, a quarterback with the Houston Texans.

Watson had signed a four-year, $156 million ($111 million guaranteed) contract extension with Houston Sept. 5, 2020. That made him the second-highest-paid quarterback in the NFL, behind only Patrick Mahomes.

"I'm lost for words, honestly" Watson said at the time of his signing. "Been crying a little bit, a lot of bit, really. It's just an amazing moment for me. The money is amazing. It's life-changing. It's great. But the biggest thing is for the (organization) to just trust in me and believe in me that I'm their guy, I'm their quarterback is the biggest thing that really touches me."

Remember the date . . . Sept. 5, 2020.

Barely mentioned in the news stories about Watson's contract extension was this: The deal included *a no-trade clause.*

I emphasize that because it became one of the most important parts of that contract for Watson . . . and one of the most damaging for the Browns.

* * *

But let's back up even a little farther.

In the 2017 NFL draft, the Browns had the No. 1 pick overall. They wisely used it to select defensive end Myles Garrett. They also had the No. 12 pick in that draft. They were still searching for a quarterback. Still available when the Browns got to No. 12 was Deshaun Watson, who had led Clemson to a national title.

Houston called the Browns. They offered the 25th pick in the 2017 draft and a first-round pick in 2018. The Browns were not sold on Watson as a franchise-changing quarterback. They were still in what they privately called the "asset acclimation" phase of team building. They were piling up draft choices.

Trading the 12th pick for the 25th plus a first-rounder in 2018? That actually is a good deal. The Browns used the 25th pick in 2017 on safety Jabrill Peppers. In 2018, the Houston first-rounder became Denzel Ward—who became a Pro Bowl cornerback.

Watson became a star in Houston. He made Pro Bowls in 2018 and 2019. After signing the 2020 contract extension, he made his third Pro Bowl. He threw for an NFL-high 4,823 yards, 33 TDs compared to only seven interceptions. Despite Watson's sizzling stats, Houston had a lot of problems and finished with a 4-12 record.

* * *

On Jan. 28, 2021, Watson demanded that Houston trade him. He vowed to sit out unless he was dealt.

This was just 4½ months after signing the contract extension and gushing about playing for the Texans.

What happened?

A rift had formed between the star quarterback and the front office over personnel changes. ESPN's Adam Schefter reported:

> By hiring former New England executive Nick Caserio to solve a large set of problems within the organization, the

> Houston Texans have created additional ones with star quarterback Deshaun Watson. Watson offered input on potential general manager candidates, but the Texans neither considered nor consulted with those endorsed by their franchise quarterback, league sources told ESPN. Additionally, the Texans did not inform Watson that they intended to hire Caserio, and he found out about the hire . . . on social media. That contributed to Watson taking to Twitter that night to post, 'some things never change. . . .'
>
> Watson's feelings were not directed toward Caserio, sources told ESPN, but instead were indicative of the way business was again conducted by the Texans. Last offseason, Houston didn't let Watson know that star wide receiver DeAndre Hopkins would be traded, which led to some disappointment. Now that it has happened again, Watson is said to be infinitely more bothered, sources told ESPN.

That and other turmoil with the Texans led to Watson's trade demand.

Houston stated that it had no plans to trade Watson.

The Browns, looking at Watson, apparently didn't consider this to be a warning sign. They should have asked themselves, *The guy signs a huge four-year contract extension and less than five months later, he wants out? Isn't that a problem?*

More was to come.

On March 16, 2021, a civil lawsuit was filed against Watson, accusing him of sexual misconduct with a massage therapist. That was only the first. More lawsuits would follow in 2021, a total of 23. Watson denied doing anything wrong.

Houston received some calls from teams inquiring about trading for Watson—before the civil lawsuits began to pile up.

The Texans set their price: three future first-round picks along with other draft assets.

* * *

Houston had a major problem with Watson. He was still threatening not to play unless he was traded. While Houston publicly said it planned to keep Watson, as the civil lawsuits and negative publicity increased, the Texans were thinking, *Maybe we better dump this guy.*

Watson, remember, had a no-trade clause in his contract. According to ESPN, as the 2021 season approached, Watson told Houston he would only approve a trade to Miami. Carolina also expressed an interest, but Watson said no to the Panthers.

Let's stop and consider this situation:

- Watson signed the four-year, $156 million contract extension Sept. 5, 2020.
- Watson asked to be traded on Jan. 28, 2021.
- Watson was hit with the first lawsuit on March 16, 2021.
- Unable or unwilling to trade Watson, Houston agreed to pay Watson his $10.5 million base salary *not* to play for the team in 2021. He worked out at the team facility, but never appeared in a game.
- By the end of the 2021 season, it was clear Watson was going to receive a significant suspension from the NFL. He also was facing possible criminal charges.

Meanwhile, the Browns had their own problems. They started the 2021 season with a 3-1 record and ended up 8-9. Baker Mayfield was playing with an injured left shoulder for most of the year—and would need surgery after the season.

When Andrew Berry talked about the "five-month odyssey" at that March 25, 2022, press conference, that meant the Browns were already seriously thinking about pursuing another quarterback in the middle of the 2021 season.

Berry and the Browns later explained the "five-month" part

of the "odyssey" wasn't simply about Mayfield. It was the time in every season when they began evaluating all the players on the roster with an eye on the following season.

That's accurate. But the deeper truth was a lack of confidence in Mayfield. Ownership wanted to deliver a first-ever Super Bowl to Cleveland's discouraged fan base. They didn't think Mayfield was the quarterback to get them there. They wanted to make a big move.

While looking at quarterbacks who might be available after the 2021 season, they didn't see their answer in the 2021 draft. Their season record wasn't going to be bad enough to guarantee a high pick. Besides, if they were going to replace Mayfield, it had to be with an established NFL quarterback who definitely was more talented.

"Once the [mid-season] trade deadline passes, you are building your free agency board and getting ready for the draft process," Berry said at the March 25, 2022 press conference. "That is when you do a lot of work on a lot of players. Given the complexity of Deshaun's situation at the time, there was going to be additional work needed to make sure to vet it as thoroughly as possible. At that time [midseason], we had made no specific decisions . . . anywhere on the roster. But we were trying to make sure we obviously had enough time to do as much research as we could."

The Browns were already seriously considering Deshaun Watson for 2022 in the middle of the 2021 football season.

SHE HAS THE BROWNS' NUMBER: ONE FAN'S STORY

There are Browns fans, and then there are Browns fans like Pauletta Hatchett.

When I thought about writing this book, people like Pauletta came to mind. These are the fans who don't just follow the team, they have a permanent residence in Browns Town. No matter how awful, even how ridiculous the Browns are in some seasons—Pauletta refuses to leave the premises.

"I grew up a Browns fan," said Hatchett. "My father took me to games in the Dawg Pound all the way back when Jim Brown and those guys were playing."

A few years ago, Pauletta told me an amazing story.

"Go ahead, ask me a name or number, anyone on the Browns," she said.

"How about Elijah Moore?" I asked.

"Number 8," she said.

"How about Jordan Akins?' I asked.

"Number 84," she said. "He played with Deshaun (Watson) in Houston. He's part of the tight end group with 85, David Njoku . . . and 88, Harrison Bryant . . . and . . ."

I just started laughing. Even though I write about the Browns, I doubt I could remember 15 of their numbers . . . although I know Joe Flacco is number 15.

At this point, you may think Pauletta is just a super fan. Some of that is true. She watches many of the online interviews with players. She reads everything she can find about the Browns.

"I prayed and fasted for D'Anthony Bell," she said.

"What's his number?" I asked.

"That's easy," she said. "He's 37. The other undrafted safety is Ronnie Hickman, number 33."

"Why were you praying for Bell?" I asked.

Pauletta explained she saw an interview with him. Bell said he and his mother were praying for him to make the team. It was a tough spot because Bell wasn't drafted.

"I identified with him," she said. "He was facing a big challenge, just like me."

Pauletta is not just some obsessive Browns fan who memorizes numbers . . . Well, she is a little obsessive. But it's more than that.

In some ways, the Browns helped her regain a certain aspect of her sanity—something few Browns fans can claim.

* * *

On Jan. 30, 2022, Pauletta was on a prayer line with several members of Akron's House of the Lord. They were asking God to care for their pastor, as Bishop Joey Johnson was facing heart surgery the next day.

"Suddenly, I had a terrible headache," she said. "I never get headaches. I didn't have any of the hypertension symptoms of people with heart problems. Suddenly, I felt so weak. I literally crawled to the bathroom to throw up."

Her son, Aaron Hatchett, was upstairs. She didn't have the strength to call out to him. She finally called him on her cellphone, and he insisted on calling 9-1-1. Pauletta was taken to the hospital where she was diagnosed with a brain aneurysm. She also had a

Can thinking about the Browns actually *help* your brain? For this fan, at least, it was life changing. *Terry Pluto*

stroke due to something called a brain asymptomatic arteriovenous malformation (AVM). According to the Mayo Clinic website, It's "a tangle of blood vessels that connects arteries and veins in the brain."

She had surgery. She had to learn to walk, to talk and to think again. She spent a month at the Edwin Shaw Rehabilitation Hospital.

"For a while, I was bed-ridden," she said. "I started on a walker, just being able to get around. I couldn't drive. I couldn't go upstairs. I'd never had a major health problem in my life until that day."

Perhaps the most frightening aspect of the ordeal for the then 67-year-old Pauletta was her failing memory and thought process.

She had worked in the information technology field for years, and later in hospital management. She's a certified grief counselor. She's ministered in 15 different countries and taught a course in "God in the workplace" at her church.

On the night of her attack, she was on the stretcher being carried out of her house. She began to wonder if she'd ever go home again.

"I looked back at the house and thought, 'I'm not going out like this. I have more life to live. I'm digging in my heels and trusting the love of the Lord,' " she said.

In April of 2022, she would have a second brain operation, something called Gamma Knife radiosurgery. According to Mayo Clinic: "It is a type of radiation therapy. It can be used to treat tumors, veins that have developed differently than usual and other differences in the brain."

That made two brain surgeries in three months.

Pauletta said she always has had a decent diet, but began to eat healthier. She worked hard on her physical therapy and her memory. She became even more emotionally invested in the Browns.

"I had to re-map my brain," she said.

* * *

While the doctors were generally pleased with her memory recovery, she knew something was missing. She and her son looked at various brain and memory exercises. They came up with their own.

"I had lost the ability to sequence and retain facts," she said. "My son Aaron has a psychology major degree and is a neuroscience minor. He knew brain function and my baseline were not normal. I had speech therapy and a lot of other therapies."

She was fighting a war on several fronts—physical, psychological, emotional and spiritual.

"One night, I was crying in my bed because I wondered if I'd ever be able to climb the stairs again," she said. "I remember hearing a preacher say, 'You can stare up at the steps . . . or you can step up to the stairs.' I got on my walker and that night, I took the first two steps on the stairs."

While she was learning to walk again and do daily chores, more was needed.

"Your brain is like a file cabinet," she said. "Everything is in there, but not in the right folders. When you try to remember things, you are looking for the right folders. I had to learn how to do that again."

Pauletta and her son needed something that aligned with her passion—something with the Browns. They decided she would memorize the Browns' roster—names and numbers. She'd also memorize it by position groups. She wanted to know about the players and coaches as people. She watched videos of rookie camp, Organized Team Activities and training camp. She watched the draft.

"At one time, I had almost a photographic memory," she said. "I had to find a way to get that back."

Then she said, "Go ahead, ask me something about the Browns."

"Name all the special teams guys," I said.

She replied: "Corey Bojorquez, 13. Dustin Hopkins, 7. Charlie Hughlett, 47. Want me to do the others?"

"Nope," I said. "That works."

But she insisted I ask more names and numbers.

I did and she got at least 20 right.

Finally, I asked, "Riley Patterson?"

"The new kicker," she said. "He's on the practice squad. He's in the 30s . . . I think, maybe 35?"

"Close enough," I said. "It's 36."

We both laughed.

* * *

Pauletta's father was a bricklayer. He loved Pauletta for many reasons, and one of their father/daughter connections was the

Browns. They watched games on TV together. They went to a few games each season and sat in the Dawg Pound.

Now the Browns are a mother/son bond.

Pauletta and Aaron watch the NFL combine . . . even taping some of it. They study videos of prospects. They read draft reports. They rate the players. They do it independently, and then compare their ratings to what happens on draft day.

I'm not making this up.

"We talk three or four times a week," she said. "We compare notes about the Browns."

The Browns became a diversion from her physical problems, along with an inspiration to overcome them.

"When Nick Chubb hurt his knee [Sept. 18, 2024, during a Browns game at Pittsburgh], I was devastated," she said. "I couldn't sleep that night. I kept praying for him. I knew what it was like to have everything physically, and then it's gone—how it changes your life."

Pauletta often talks about the various Browns players coming back from surgeries. She mentions how so many people prayed for her. Pauletta is a certified grief counselor and a mental health fitness instructor. She has helped people deal with trauma, losing a loved one and brain issues.

She knows there's more to life than the Browns. But she also learned how the Browns—even with all their losing—make her life better.

BIGGEST DEAL EVER: DESHAUN WATSON COMES TO CLEVELAND

When word leaked out that the Browns were one of four teams set to meet with Deshaun Watson, I wrote a column begging the team not to be involved.

His holdout in Houston less than five months after signing a four-year contract extension . . .

The 20-plus civil suits charging him with sexual misconduct . . .

Although trade details had not been yet announced, word was it would involve multiple first-round draft picks going to Houston.

The process worked like this: Before a team could talk to Watson about waiving his no-trade clause, that team first had to work a deal with the Texans.

Four teams were willing to meet Houston's price for Watson: Carolina, New Orleans, Atlanta and Cleveland.

Watson and his lawyer Rusty Hardin set up separate videoconference meetings with each team interested in Watson. According to a story by The Athletic's Jason Lloyd, Watson's quarterbacks coach and friend Quincy Avery and his agent David Mulugheta also were part of the meeting.

For their meeting, the Browns' party included team owners Dee and Jimmy Haslam, head coach Kevin Stefanski and GM Andrew Berry.

Watson's lawyer, Hardin, not only was defending Watson in the various civil suits filed against him, he also was close to the Haslams. He had represented the family's Pilot/Flying J truck stop business when it ran into legal trouble.

The company agreed to pay $92 million to the federal government in 2014 for defrauding trucking companies buying gasoline. Another estimated $85 million was paid to customers who were damaged by the fraudulent business practices. The Haslam family was never charged or found to be at fault when the investigation was completed.

Hardin's law firm had already guided the Haslams through one difficult legal situation. Now Hardin was on the other side of the table, there to help Watson with his legal problems.

"We knew Rusty (Hardin) just a little bit from the Pilot situation," Jimmy Haslam said at the Watson press conference. "We obviously spent a lot of time with him and his legal team as we worked through the process with Deshaun."

Hardin assured the Browns that Watson would not—at least to his knowledge—face any criminal charges. This was the Browns' main concern. Had Watson been charged in a criminal court, the Browns would have dropped their quest for Watson. But Watson was not indicted by grand juries in Brazoria County and one in Harris County that heard evidence.

"Two different grand juries in two different counties looked at nine different criminal cases and decided not to go forward," said Jimmy Haslam. "We have decided to trust the process."

In their March 25, 2022, press conference announcing the acquisition of Watson, the Browns discussed how they "vetted" the quarterback. Berry said:

> We used independent investigative resources within the Harris County and Houston law enforcement community in order to get an unbiased, well-rounded and comprehensive

> perspective on the allegations. We did not want it just to be one-sided. We used third-party legal counsel that allowed us to really analyze . . . all of the information that we were able to collect and amass.
>
> I should note because I know a lot has been said about this, we were advised by our attorneys—we were advised against reaching out directly to the 22 women out of concern that it would be considered interfering with the criminal investigation. . . .
>
> It was through this time and through this work and what we learned about Deshaun the person and what we learned about the civil and criminal proceedings and obviously working through due process and legal process that got us comfortable with Deshaun the person.
>
> We realize and we are not naive to the fact that there are many people who are not as comfortable with this transaction as we are today, but this is something that is a trade that we made to be evaluated over the long run, we do think that there is a strong and detailed body of work about Deshaun and we do have faith in him as a person.

The Browns and the Haslams talked about having had in-depth conversations with women who worked for the team along with female friends and family members to elicit their thoughts on the Browns signing Watson. In the end, the Browns thought they believed in Watson enough to move ahead with the acquisition.

* * *

When I heard four different teams were meeting with Watson, I assumed it was for the teams to get to know the quarterback. It was a chance for Watson to explain his side of the civil lawsuits and stories about his conduct with massage therapists.

That did happen. And Watson denied any misbehavior.

I'm told that the message he gave the Browns and other teams who interviewed him was essentially the same as the statement he made later during the March 25, 2022 press conference with the Browns:

> I know these allegations are very, very serious. I've never assaulted any woman. I've never disrespected any woman. I was raised by a single-parent mom, who has two aunties as her sisters—and that is who raised me. I was raised to be genuine. I respect everyone and everything around me.

In his mind, he had done nothing wrong.

Later, while Watson spent time with Kevin Stefanski talking football, the business conversation continued with Berry, the Haslams and Watson's representatives. This meeting turned into a contract renegotiation.

Perhaps I'm naive, but when I heard this, I was outraged. Here was a guy who was facing multiple civil lawsuits. The negative publicity attached to his name was upsetting many who follow football. He had sat out the entire 2021 season. He still had three more years on that original contract . . . and his agents had pressed for a *new contract?*

Not only that, teams were willing to give it to him.

The advantage should have been with the teams willing to bring in Watson and endure the certain harsh public relations backlash. But that was not the case here.

* * *

Watson didn't even want to play in Cleveland.

The only time he had faced the Browns on the shores of Lake Erie was Nov. 15, 2020. The game was delayed for 36 minutes because of a thunderstorm, with hail and wind gusts up to 40 mph. Although the temperature was in the 50s, the wind made it feel much colder.

The Browns beat Houston, 10-7. Watson threw for only 163 yards, his lowest output of that 2020 Pro Bowl season. In every other game, he threw for at least 219 yards.

Watson grew up in the South. High school football in the Atlanta area. College football at Clemson in South Carolina. Pro football with Houston in a dome. He was not a quarterback who wanted to play in wild weather. Consider the other three teams besides the Browns who were bidding for him: Carolina, New Orleans and Atlanta. Not only are New Orleans and Atlanta in the south, they also play in domed stadiums.

Atlanta was Watson's favorite. He wanted to lead his hometown Falcons back to the playoffs after they had endured four losing seasons in a row. His friend and quarterbacks coach Quincy Avery was based in Atlanta.

Carolina was eliminated. The Panthers reportedly didn't want to give Watson a fully guaranteed four-year contract.

The Browns, too, were told they were out. But they didn't give up. Berry kept in contact with Watson's agent.

Soon, the Watson camp realized the Browns were willing to out-bid Atlanta and anyone else.

Watson actually liked meeting with the Browns. He began to reconsider Cleveland, especially as the Browns pushed so hard to sign him.

At his press conference, I asked Watson why he originally turned down Cleveland and then changed his mind to sign with the Browns.

"It was not necessarily a turn down," Watson said. "The media was kind of rushing me to make a decision. I was not comfortable making that . . . decision. The news gets out and things like that . . . I knew that Cleveland was the best situation from a football standpoint and a family atmosphere."

Watson played the "media card," which often happens in situations like this.

As the Browns' newest QB spoke to the media on March 25, 2022, nobody seemed comfortable—including GM Andrew Berry (left) and head coach Kevin Stefanski (right). *David Petkiewicz / cleveland.com*

"[Coming to Cleveland] had nothing to do with the contract," Watson said. "I did not know about the contract until I told my agent I wanted to come and be a Cleveland Brown. That [the contract] was secondary. That was after the fact . . . that had nothing to do with me choosing the Cleveland Browns."

Most of the time, a player signs a huge contract and then insists "It had nothing to do with the money."

So Watson's comments weren't original.

But the contract . . . *the contract* . . . THE CONTRACT!

The contract was a five-year, $230 million *fully guaranteed* deal . . . the largest of its kind in NFL history to that point.

Sports agents keep score. Notice the $230 million guaranteed over five years. Why $230 million? Why not $225 million, an average of $45 million a year? That's because star Kansas City quarterback Patrick Mahomes was making an average of $45 million a year. Watson's new deal put him at $46 million a year—and gave him the largest guaranteed deal.

* * *

The press conference at which the Browns introduced Deshaun Watson was grim. Really, really grim. The media room was far more quiet than usual. When Browns GM Andrew Berry and coach Kevin Stefanski walked to the table with Watson, they knew this was going to be one of their toughest press conferences ever.

Berry and Stefanski looked like they were headed to the hospital for a colonoscopy. They just wanted to get this over with. When they stood next to Watson as he held up his new No. 4 Browns jersey, Berry and Stefanski couldn't even fake a smile. Watson did his best to look pleased, but no one seemed happy.

It's the opposite of what you'd normally expect when a team makes a huge trade for a three-time Pro Bowl quarterback . . . especially a quarterback-starved franchise such as the Browns.

But nothing was normal about the Browns' pursuit and signing of Watson. The Browns already were receiving complaints from fans and scourging from the media because of the civil suits and lurid media accounts of Watson's activity with massage therapists that had been made public.

Peter King of NBC.com sports wrote: "I don't think any team should go into business with a player—though cleared of criminal charges—who has 22 women accusing him of indecent acts . . . (where else) would a person with such serious accusations against him be handed a guaranteed $230 million to lead the jewel of the community, a prized and beloved public trust like the Cleveland Browns."

The Browns were fixated on one thing: bringing in Watson—almost regardless of the cost. They believed it was worth the bad publicity because they believed he'd be a great quarterback.

"We think he is one of the best players at the position in this sport," GM Andrew Berry said at Watson's introductory press conference. "It became pretty straightforward . . . He's obviously in his prime. We think it's the most important position in this sport. Once we were able to get comfortable with him as a person, the football part in terms of the evaluation was easy."

Meanwhile, Watson said things like "I continue to say I am a servant leader because I wrote a book on it. That was how I was before any of these allegations."

Watson was talking about a book called *Pass It On: Work Hard, Serve Others . . . Repeat,* which he wrote with Lavelle Lavette and that was published right before the 2020 season.

Watson also insisted he would "continue to fight for my name and clear my name . . . I never did the things that these people are alleging."

He said he had no plans to receive counseling.

"I do not have a problem," he said. "I don't have an issue. I've been saying that from the beginning . . . I never assaulted anyone. I never disrespected anyone."

I asked Watson about using more than 40 massage therapists. Most pro athletes are very picky when allowing people to work on their bodies.

"Forty is just over the time," said Watson. "It's not in one period of time. I have been in Houston for five years and you go to different people . . . you kind of meet different people over time."

It was a poor answer, and even Watson seemed to know it. Any team would be happy to connect their players with the best therapist available.

This press conference was almost cringe-worthy at times because of the discussion of massage therapists, civil suits and women who have dealt with sexual assaults in their past.

That was how the Browns brought in their new quarterback.

* * *

Here's what I wrote immediately after the trade:

> The Browns are bringing Deshaun Watson to Cleveland. That's shocking enough, given how Watson originally turned down the Browns.
>
> But this?
>
> The Browns are sending three first-round picks and three lower draft picks to Houston as part of the trade. They are giving him a fully guaranteed $230 million contract—highest in NFL history.
>
> I can't decide if I'm outraged or speechless.
>
> Or both.
>
> The Browns just guaranteed the most money in NFL history to a guy who didn't even play last season because of his legal problems dealing with alleged sexual-assault cases. While no criminal charges will be filed, there are still 22 civil claims pending.
>
> Furthermore, he possibly will be suspended for some games to open this season.
>
> Giving up salary cap space . . .
>
> Future draft assets . . .
>
> A contract larger (in guarantees) than those recently given to Patrick Mahomes, Aaron Rodgers and Josh Allen?
>
> What kind of analytics is this?
>
> I'll answer my own question: It's desperation.

* * *

The Browns were embarrassed with the initial rejection by Watson, who obviously didn't want to come to Cleveland. He was trying to decide between New Orleans and Atlanta.

That's worth remembering. So when he arrives and finally speaks publicly, Watson had better not say, "It's not about the money."

The contract was a five-year, $230 million fully guaranteed deal . . . the largest of its kind in NFL history to that point. *John Kuntz / cleveland.com*

It's all about the money.

Those who like bold moves will say the Browns deserve credit for refusing to be rejected—so they decided to make him an offer he couldn't refuse.

It's an offer so unprecedented I thought it was a joke when the initial reports hit Twitter.

It's not.

It's a belief by the Browns that Watson will transform the franchise and be the QB Cleveland has wanted since the days of Bernie Kosar in the late 1980s.

Maybe that happens, but I have major doubts.

* * *

As I'm writing this, I'm receiving texts and emails from friends and readers.

The vast majority of the fan base didn't want to enter into

the unsavory business of trying to bring Watson to town on his original contract.

"I'm done," wrote one fan.

Granted, Browns fans swear off the team seemingly every year.

But this is a little different. The female fan base will be hit especially hard by this decision. There are real moral considerations about this decision.

My guess, the Browns know this.

My guess is they don't care—or at least, they don't care enough to back away from Watson.

They are gambling the team will win enough games and the fans will accept Watson or anyone else who delivers a team consistently into the playoffs.

That could be true.

But giving this guy a huge raise? I can't get past that right now. Nor can I comprehend all the draft picks and salary cap consequences involved in the deal.

Finally, I can't recall the last time I was so angered and disappointed by a decision by a local franchise.

* * *

Nothing that happened after signing Watson changed my opinion. If anything, the results were even worse than I expected.

FANS WRITE IN ABOUT THE DESHAUN WATSON DEAL

When the Browns acquired Deshaun Watson, I was ashamed and angered. I made a donation to the Cleveland rape crisis center. My enthusiasm for the Browns is about 10% of what it was before the deal. The football impact has been disastrous for the Browns, but the moral stain this trade left on the franchise will never go away.

— Craig Swarts, Columbus, Ohio

I packed up all my Browns memorabilia, hats and jerseys. I taped the boxes up, labeled them "Do Not Open Until Watson is gone" and put them in the shed. I never could have predicted it would have gone so bad. I really don't know if the team will ever recover. Truly sad.

— John Moosey, Fishhook, Alaska

The Browns gave up way too much and paid too much for what they should have known would be a horrible marketing move in the Cleveland community with his polarizing legal issues. It was doomed from the start, and we see how it ended. It was an unmitigated disaster, and I am not sure how the Front Office remains unscathed to date.

— Jeff McConnell, Bowling Green, Ohio

When the Browns acquired Deshaun Watson, I actually was pretty happy. I have this theory: if you look at the betting, there is rarely a point spread above 8 in the NFL. This means most games will come down to one possession. And you have to have that guy that can win a game in the fourth quarter. You already know the names of the guys that can do it. Baker Mayfield didn't come to mind. So I was convinced they needed someone else. I was excited to get a guy just entering his prime that had the tools to be great.

— Mike Case, Tallmadge, Ohio

When the Browns traded for Watson, I of course felt morally conflicted, but never once did it even cross my mind that Watson would be anything short of a very good quarterback, if not an elite one. I overrode my moral concerns by (correctly I believe) saying that any team in the Browns situation would have made that trade regardless of the allegations, and that numerous other teams were actively pursuing Watson. I really felt the Browns finally had a good quarterback, even if they took a shortcut to get there, and it never even crossed my mind that his level of play would be any sort of concern.

— Tyler Lance, Algona, Iowa

When the Browns acquired Watson I had a hard time separating the accusations from the sporting accomplishments of this guy. As much as I wanted to root for him there was this small part of me that wondered if the charges on him were true. Unfortunately for him I think he was highly distracted from football over that and when it was revealed that he was lax in his recovery I lost a ton of respect for him.

— John Tomasko, Frisco, Texas

I was so desperate to see the Browns be a good team that my initial reaction to it [the Deshaun Watson deal] was excitement. I didn't care about the picks, the contract — and figured there were plenty of other bad guys in the NFL and that the off-field stuff would blow over. But once I had to talk to my wife about it, then my kids, then my non-Browns friends, I was no longer into it. That trade has made it so hard to be fan—worse than going 1-31.

— Joe Valponi, Columbus, Ohio

When the Browns acquired Deshaun Watson in 2022, I felt like he was the final piece of the puzzle. At that point the Browns were built to WIN NOW. All we needed was the franchise QB. I was willing to ignore the off-the-field issues as we needed a true franchise QB.

— Michael McSweeney, San Diego, California

ONE OF THE GREAT "WHAT IFS?": BAKER MAYFIELD

Baker Mayfield.

Just mentioning the name angers many Browns fans.

They're not upset *at* Mayfield.

It's the Browns.

What if . . . the Browns had just kept Mayfield?

What if . . . the Browns had just been patient with Mayfield, given him a chance to have shoulder surgery and come back healthy in 2022?

What if . . . the Browns never signed Deshaun Watson and didn't trade all the draft picks, etc.? (That's right, keeping Mayfield would have meant no Watson in Cleveland.)

Baker Mayfield had a lot of fans in Cleveland, despite his rocky 2021 season (detailed in a previous chapter).

Think about Mayfield's four seasons in Cleveland.

He went through four head coaches (Hue Jackson, Gregg Williams, Freddie Kitchens and Kevin Stefanski). He had four offensive coordinators (Todd Haley, Kitchens, Todd Monken and Alex Van Pelt).

Despite all the coaching chaos—and a significant shoulder injury in 2021—he still had a 29-30 record as a starter. He ranked behind only Otto Graham, Brian Sipe and Bernie Kosar in all-time passing yardage by Browns quarterbacks.

Many Browns fans wonder why the team continued to play Mayfield when he was bothered with an injured (non-throwing) left shoulder. That shoulder eventually required surgery after the season.

And why not give him another chance in 2022 after the operation?

That's a legitimate question. The Browns told me they would indeed have done that had Watson not become available. But Houston wanted to dump Watson, and Watson inspired in the Browns visions of Super Bowl grandeur despite all of his flaws.

Three years after Watson signed with the Browns and Mayfield was traded to Carolina, one of those two quarterbacks had led his team to a pair of playoff appearances.

Three years later . . . One of those two quarterbacks had been to the Pro Bowl—twice.

Three years later . . . The decision to trade for and sign Watson to the rich contract looked even worse for Cleveland—because of what Mayfield has done in that span.

* * *

After the Browns signed Watson, they traded Mayfield to Carolina for a fifth-round draft pick.

Mayfield's career was in trouble.

Why say that? The Browns offered him all over the NFL, and only Carolina was willing to take a chance on him. (And that was mostly because the Browns basically gave him away and paid $10 million of his $18.8 million salary).

The Browns had offered Mayfield to Houston in the Watson deal. The Texans wanted no part of him. They were willing to lose a bunch of games in 2022 by basically playing with unproven quarterbacks. The idea was to secure a high draft pick.

Just when it seemed like the Browns had finally gotten it right . . . Myles Garrett and Baker Mayfield celebrate beating the Steelers in a wild-card playoff game. Might there have been more celebrations like this?
Joshua Gunter / cleveland.com

Mayfield could have been the NFL's version of a scratch-off lottery ticket. Really, what did any team have to lose because the Browns just wanted to unload him. But word across the NFL was that Mayfield's ego was far larger than his talent. He also was viewed as someone who clashed with coaches. Not all of that is fair, but it hurt his trade value.

Carolina was the exception because the Panthers were 5-12. They had an 0-5 record with Cam Newton as a starter. Their other starter was Sam Darnold (4-7 record). That's the same Sam Darnold who was the No. 3 pick in 2018—the same draft in which Mayfield was the No. 1 pick.

In 2022, Mayfield bounced from Carolina to the Los Angeles

Rams. He had a 2-8 record as a starter. He threw 10 touchdown passes compared to eight interceptions. That season looked a lot like Mayfield's dismal 2021 performance with the Browns.

Between 2021 and 2022, Mayfield had an 8-16 record as a starter with 27 touchdown passes, 21 interceptions. He was headed down the road of being a career NFL backup, drifting from team to team. After all, he went through three teams in two years.

Next stop was Tampa Bay in 2023, where he replaced . . . Tom Brady? That's right, Tom Brady. In 2022, the Bucs were 8-9 in Brady's final season. The Bucs signed Mayfield to a one-year contract, with $4 million guaranteed. He could earn up to $8.5 million with incentives.

It was almost a last-chance contract. It was low risk to the team, a huge drop from Mayfield's $18.8 million salary in 2022.

The Bucs gave Mayfield a fresh start with a new team that had some talent. They were 9-8 with Mayfield in 2023. He played all 17 games. Tampa Bay made the playoffs and beat Philadelphia 32-9 in the first round.

Mayfield had a season much like he had when helping the Browns to the 2020 playoffs and a first-round victory over Pittsburgh. In that 2020 Cleveland season, Mayfield threw 26 TD passes compared to eight interceptions. He completed 63% of his passes.

For the Bucs, Mayfield threw 28 touchdown passes compared to 10 interceptions, completing 64% of his passes.

Mayfield's supporters always believed there was a solid starting NFL quarterback inside him. He had some maturity issues. He also battled injuries. But the fact was Mayfield had some success in Cleveland. That 2020 season was terrific. Mayfield adapted to coach Kevin Stefanski's more disciplined offense. In 2019 with Freddie Kitchens as head coach, an undisciplined Mayfield threw 21 interceptions. In 2020, that total fell to eight. His touchdown passes rose from 22 to 26.

After the 2023 season, Mayfield was headed to free agency, but

What if the Browns had just been patient with Baker Mayfield, given him a chance to have shoulder surgery and come back healthy in 2022?
Joshua Gunter / cleveland.com

Tampa Bay made sure he stayed with the team, signing him to a three-year, $100 million deal ($50 million guaranteed).

Mayfield responded in 2024, leading the Bucs to a 10-7 record and another playoff spot. He threw 41 touchdown passes. He did lead the NFL with 16 interceptions. He had a 106.8 QB rating, the highest of his career.

Mayfield also helped two Tampa offensive coordinators become head coaches. Dave Canales left Tampa after the 2023 season to become head coach of Carolina. His replacement, Liam Coen, after one season was hired in 2025 to be the head coach in Jacksonville.

Baker Mayfield, a guy whose own NFL career was in jeopardy heading into the 2023 season, suddenly became a quarterback who launched first-time head NFL coaching careers for his last two offensive coordinators.

* * *

Would Mayfield have had this success in Cleveland?

My answer is . . . I don't know.

I do believe the Browns would have been wise to keep Mayfield for another year. That's not a second guess. I wrote it the moment the Browns began their pursuit of Watson.

But Mayfield struggled in 2022. He went to Carolina, a lousy team. He also had some injuries. He was cut by Carolina and picked up by the Rams. He had a few nice moments for Rams head coach Sean McVay, but his record was 1-3 as a starter. The Rams did not make an effort to re-sign him even as a backup.

Tampa Bay appeared to be Mayfield's last chance in the NFL . . . and he knew it. Always brash before, he had been humbled. He knew the Browns paid Carolina to take him. He knew that Carolina tried to trade him, and no one was interested. He knew something had to change.

"He went through a rough patch early in his career," Tampa Bay GM Jason Licht told ESPN in an interview after the 2024 season. "But he felt like he was wanted [in Tampa Bay]. He was wanted by the head coach, the GM, the coaching staff and the players. We wanted him. There's a psychological advantage to that once [a quarterback] feels like he's at a place where everybody wants him."

Most adults don't make major changes in their lives without enduring at least some type of physical or emotional pain. Mayfield dealt with both.

What if the Browns had kept Mayfield? Hard to know if he'd have had the same success as in Tampa. But at least Cleveland would have found out—and would not have had to endure the problems his replacement brought to the franchise.

FANS WRITE IN ABOUT BAKER MAYFIELD . . .

Baker Mayfield was treated unfairly, as he was blamed for his poor play while injured but would have been called "soft" for not playing.

— Jeremy Weiss, Herndon, Virginia

I did not want Baker Mayfield originally. He won me over time with his energy and what seemed to be a genuine attachment to Cleveland. Now I root for Baker and am happy to see him succeed. I think he is one of those people that if you count them out, they set out to prove you were wrong. And the Browns were wrong.

— Holly Monte, North Canton

By trying to play through the injury because of contract reasons, Baker's selfishness hurt himself and the team. He lost the locker room. It was time for him to move on. A mentor once told me, "Sometimes getting fired is the best thing that can happen to you." I think that was the case with Baker.

— John Spearman, Round Pond, Maine

I thought the Browns made the right move drafting Baker Mayfield in 2018. Although a gamer, he was immature. Then he wore out his welcome. It was time for him to go. You now see his potential. But that would have never happened in Cleveland. I believe being humbled in Carolina set the tone for his success. Happy he's doing well.

— Doug Carr, Titusville, Pennsylvania

I hated Baker Mayfield when they drafted him because of the flag planting at Ohio State and because I was actually high on Josh Allen in that year's draft. I also prefer my professional athletes to lean more toward the "professional" side of behavior. I thought that Baker was too "me-centered" and trying too hard to get attention. However, that man gave every ounce of his body to the Browns while here. If he had not been so recklessly devoted to playing football "the right way," he probably would never have gotten hurt and I believe he would have received that second contract with the Browns. I think that Baker Mayfield is a guy that, you want in the foxhole with you, so to speak.

— Shawn Colin Bailey Sr., Mileses, New York

As an Ohio State fan, I hated Baker initially, but stayed hopeful. He definitely had his ups and downs, but I came to be a big fan, and still like him to this day. He brought a swagger to Cleveland it felt like we had never had. Even if he wasn't elite, it felt like we just threw him away because he didn't win a Super Bowl, even though he led us to the most successful season we had seen in a very long time. I'll probably always be a Baker fan.

— Alec Thomas, Bucyrus, Ohio

I like Baker Mayfield. He had some immaturity, but he played hard nosed football. He had so much confidence in his arm. He sometimes made the wrong decision, but I thought the Browns could help him with that.

— Scott Hanna, Avon, Ohio

Baker Mayfield I liked from the start because he seemed willing to do what no one else wanted to do, not sure if it was bravery, hope, idealism or just plain being a glutton for punishment, but it aligned with all the feelings I've come to know over the last 50 years as Browns football season lol. I love my Browns, always have and always will, but we know it's not for the weak. I'll likely always like Mayfield because of his attitude and his character.

— Elke Sündermann, Cleveland, Ohio

The way the Browns gave up on Baker Mayfield and chose Watson made me want to see Mayfield succeed. You could tell Cleveland didn't really want him after a point—even though Mayfield's underdog swagger and attitude fit the grittiness of Cleveland. He's no longer a Brown, but he deserves our respect.

— Bill Melville, Colorado Springs, Colorado

I'm in my 80s now and have turned into a big Browns football viewer and fan. If they are playing on a Sunday, I will cancel plans to go polka dancing and stay home to cheer. When my husband was alive and watching football on TV, I would find some excuse to exit and go shopping. I think my interest started with Baker Mayfield. I loved his attitude, upbeat personality. I will never understand why the head office doesn't ask the opinion of the average grandmother to help pick the next QB.

— Barbara Trcka, Hinckley, Ohio

THE BEST SINCE JIM BROWN: NICK CHUBB

Jim Donovan, the Browns' great radio voice, was in the hospital receiving a new round of treatments for leukemia when he told this story about the 2023 season.

"I did the opener [Sept. 10, 2023]," Donovan said. "Then I stepped away [from the broadcast]. At that point, I didn't know if I could come back again [that season]. I don't think a lot of the people treating me thought that could happen."

Donovan had been battling chronic lymphocytic leukemia (CLL) since 2000, when he was first diagnosed. He also had melanoma along the way. By the summer of 2023, he knew more treatments were needed. His goal was to call the opening game, which he did as the Browns beat Cincinnati, 24-3.

Then, he went into the hospital.

"A lot of people were telling me, 'There's always next year. You'll feel better by then,' " said Donovan. "That was disheartening because I wanted to come back this year."

Donovan was in his hospital room watching the Browns' loss to the Steelers 26-22 on Monday Night Football.

"That was the first game I was going to miss," said Donovan. "It was one of my saddest days. I always loved going to Pittsburgh. It's

Nick Chubb in his prime (here, in 2020) was hard to catch and even harder to stop. He ranks third on the Browns' all-time rushing list, after Jim Brown and Leroy Kelly. *Joshua Gunter / cleveland.com*

such great theater over there—even though it usually didn't come out well for the Browns."

Instead, Donovan was in the hospital, his head filled with the plans for various treatments—many of them were going to wear down his body and drain him emotionally. His main treatment was CAR T-cell therapy, a new way to fight cancer.

"I was watching the game, and Nick Chubb went down with a knee injury," said Donovan. "I'm really sad. I got up, went to the TV and turned down the volume. Then I started to do my own play-by-play from the hospital room."

Donovan already was depressed during his battle with leukemia. Then he saw Chubb, one of his favorite players, suffer a devastating knee surgery. Rather than shut down and slip deeper into depression, Donovan began announcing the game. He didn't want to give up, just as he knew Chubb would battle back from whatever was coming next. This was therapy for Donovan. He continued to do it while he was off the air, calling those games just as if he were in the booth. People walking down the hospital hallways would stop in his room and listen.

"I was in the hospital for three weeks," he said. "Some people said, 'Hey, you sound great!' I'd thank them and then tell them to shut the door."

The way Donovan told the story, we both ended up laughing.

But I think about that story now and my heart breaks. Donovan passed away from leukemia and some other forms of cancer on Oct. 26, 2024.

Donovan grew up in Boston, so he never watched Jim Brown play in person. He thought Nick Chubb was the best running back he ever saw in a Browns uniform.

I agreed—except for one man.

Jim Brown.

You have to be in the Medicare generation to have watched Brown play live. But in the modern media generation, you can find videos online. I challenge anyone to find a running back who can match Jim Brown.

The first thing you'll probably notice is Brown carried the football like a loaf of bread. At times, he held it in one hand, far away from his body. When Brown was in the backfield and running a sweep behind pulling guards Gene Hickerson and John Wooten, he would hold the football in one of his huge hands. He used the other hand to swat away opposing tacklers, much like someone pushing aside an annoying puppy.

No coach would want a player to carry a football like Brown. It would seem to be an invitation to fumble. But no coach ever had a running back quite like Jim Brown. Not when you combined the power, the speed and the controlled anger that he unleashed during his nine seasons with the Browns.

Tough-minded Cleveland head coach Paul Brown had to hate it

when his running back defied basic football fundamentals by gripping the football as Jim Brown did. But Paul Brown didn't say a word. He realized Jim Brown wouldn't listen. Jim Brown also never missed a game. He rarely missed practice.

Jim Brown—the greatest Cleveland Brown ever. I'll make the case Jim Brown was the greatest NFL running back ever. He rushed for 106 touchdowns. He caught 20 TD passes, meaning he had more touchdowns (126) than games played (118). Brown played nine NFL seasons and led the league in rushing eight times. He averaged an NFL record 104 yards rushing per game for his career. No running back was ever so dominant in his era.

* * *

New England coach Bill Belichick once told me that Paul Brown was the greatest NFL coach ever. Perhaps you agree. But did you know that Paul Brown went into the 1957 NFL draft *not* looking to select Jim Brown, the star running back from Syracuse?

Paul Brown wanted a quarterback. He had two on his list—John Brodie and Len Dawson. Cleveland had the No. 6 pick in the draft. Brodie went No. 3, Dawson was selected at No. 5. Paul Brown liked Jim Brown. To the coach's credit, he didn't try to force the issue by drafting another quarterback. He took Jim Brown.

And two guys with the last name of Brown worked magic for a team called the Cleveland Browns. Jim Brown is in the Hall of Fame. You probably knew that, as in the Pro Football Hall of Fame.

Brown also is in the National Lacrosse of Hall of Fame. He is considered one of the greatest college lacrosse players ever. In 1957—the same year he was drafted by the Browns—Jim Brown scored five goals in the first half of the college North/South Lacrosse All-Star game.

The 1957 Syracuse lacrosse team was 10-0. Brown was a first-team All-American in lacrosse.

Then there was basketball.

The 6-foot-2 Brown played two years of that sport, averaging 13.1 points. He also ran track.

Let's add it up: All-American in football. All-American in lacrosse. A star in track. A starter in basketball.

That's right, Brown played four sports at an elite level at college powerhouse Syracuse. Oh, the Yankees also were interested in signing him to a baseball contract.

When I was writing the book *Browns Town 1964*, several members of the 1964 championship team told me "Jim Brown was the only guy Paul Brown couldn't intimidate."

Paul Brown was an old-school coach when old-school was in school during the post–World War II era of pro football. The coach's film sessions were brutal. Big men such as star defensive end Bill Glass said Paul Brown could use the film to bring embarrassed tears to your eyes.

But the coach didn't do that with Jim Brown. He pointed out mistakes, but in a non-threatening way.

Paul Brown never did things like take the running back out of the game after a mistake, and then walk up to him and say, "Don't tell me the great ones did it that way."

That was one of Paul Brown's methods of motivating players, and humbling them at the same time.

Not with Jim Brown.

Jim Brown once told me the thing he admired most about Paul Brown was "how he integrated the team and the roommates. He never said a word. He posted the rooming list, a black player with a white player. He just did it."

Jim Brown battled Paul Brown on play calling. The coach liked to run Brown up the middle. Brown wanted more sweeps.

The 6-foot-2, 235-pound Brown had a fullback's power with a sprinter's speed. Let's put his weight of 235 in perspective. When he played in the NFL, many linemen were in the 250-pound range, some even lighter.

Nick Chubb is taken off the field after injuring his leg in the first half during Monday Night Football, Sept. 18, 2023, in Pittsburgh.
Joshua Gunter / cleveland.com

It's hard to find a story about Jim Brown's time in the 40-yard dash. A New York Times piece said the "legend" was 4.5. Not especially fast by today's standards. But he supposedly started out of a 3-point football stance.

Besides, it's irrelevant. Do you know when Jim Brown was the fastest? When someone was chasing him on the football field.

Nick Chubb was much the same way in his best days with the Browns. Forget the stopwatch; send a linebacker or safety after him and see who runs faster.

Jim Brown loved it when a single tackler tried to bring him down. Brown would use his legs like pistons, knocking the defender away much like a big brother dismissing a little brother's feeble attempt to bring him to the ground. When Jim Brown was tackled, he seemed to take forever to stand back up. Then he dragged himself back to the huddle. You'd swear he'd never be able to take another step. Then they'd hand him the ball, and he'd run over and past anyone trying to get in his way.

Scoring a touchdown brought no emotion from Brown. He simply handed the ball to the official, and headed to the sideline like a guy leaving the assembly line to take a break for a few minutes.

* * *

When Nick Chubb—now a former Brown—signed with the Houston Texans on June 8, 2025, that inspired me to think about Chubb and Jim Brown.

Both are sons of the South.

Brown was born Feb. 17, 1936, on St. Simons Island, a Georgia coastal town between Savannah and Jacksonville, Florida. The St. Simons of his youth was warm breezes off the Atlantic. It was piercing blue skies. It was pure white sand under his feet and seagulls flying overhead. It was palm trees. It was sometimes spotting a few dolphins offshore. In the late 1930s and early 1940s. Much of the island was still being farmed, sometimes by men with plows pulled by horses.

"It was another world," Jim Brown told me when I interviewed him about 20 years ago.

When Brown was 2 years old, his mother moved to Great Neck, New York to find work as a maid. This was 1938, the Depression still crushing working people. Brown remained in St. Simons, living with his grandmother and his aunt.

His father was Swinton "Sweet Sue" Brown, who was seldom in the life of his son. He left Brown's mother soon after Jim was born.

"It was said he was impossible to dislike," Brown wrote in his book, *Off My Chest*. "It just happened that he had a weakness for dice and cards."

A gambler and a lady's man, Swinton Brown also went North not long after his son was born. One news report said Swinton Brown died in 1958 and Jim Brown didn't attend the funeral.

Brown's family were the women of St. Simons—a great-grandmother, a grandmother, a couple of aunts. He was educated in what he called "a two-room schoolhouse where one teacher handled all the elementary grades." This was the Jim Crow South, where African Americans had their own churches, schools, businesses and stores.

"We had our own self-contained community," said Brown. "It was a good way to grow up."

Nearby Sea Island was a vacation spot for the wealthy. As Brown said, "I was very aware there were places I shouldn't go."

When Jim Brown turned 8, he moved to Manhasset, New York, on Long Island, to join his mother. She made sure her son stayed with a friend and a butler who lived near Manhasset High School. She wanted her son to attend the mostly white school because of its strong academics.

"We lived on the dividing line," Brown told Manhasset students during a 2013 speech at the school. "She wanted me to come here. She used a little trickery."

Brown played five high school sports and earned 13 letters. He was a superstar in virtually everything, from football to lacrosse to track and basketball, where he averaged 38 points one season. As a senior, he averaged 15 yards per carry. That's right, 15 yards!

Brown graduated with a B average. One of his coaches gave him an IQ test to prove he had what it takes to excel in the classroom. They told him to use sports to get an education. A couple of Syracuse graduates who taught at the high school convinced him to attend their alma mater.

* * *

Nicholas Jamal Chubb has his roots in Chubbtown, Georgia, near the Alabama state line. The people who started the town were free African Americans who migrated to Georgia from North Carolina.

"According to records of Floyd County, where Chubbtown is located, Henry Chub (spelled with one b), one of the original eight sons, purchased 120 acres for $900 in 1864, before the end of the Civil War," wrote cleveland.com's Scott Patsko. "The settlement grew to include a church, school, post office, meeting hall and a lodge. It also had businesses such as a sawmill, cotton gin, wagon company, blacksmith, grist mill, syrup mill and a company that made caskets. The settlers farmed the land and were self-sufficient."

The town of about 200 people was destroyed in the Big Cedar flood in 1916. Chubb grew up in Cedartown, Georgia, about 6 miles from the original Chubbtown. It's 75 miles northwest of Atlanta.

In a 2024 Players Tribune story, Nick Chubb wrote about his mother's side of the family:

> [My mother] raised me, and she was on her own for most of my childhood . . . My mom worked her ass off just to provide for us. She was working double shifts from when I was super young. I used to sneak down from our bedroom and see her crying over bills late at night. Like you see in the movies. That was our real life. . . . Just super poor, super stressed all the time. When I was around 10, my mom took on an extra night shift, and so we moved in with our grandma.
>
> And my grandma. . . . How can I say this without her taking it the wrong way? Because I *love* my grandma. My grandma was super strict. *Super.* She took no mess. When the sun went down at night, we had to stop laughing.
>
> "At six o'clock the laughin' stops."
>
> That was the rule. Because once the sun went down, that meant it was time to get serious and start thinking about your work the next day. But we were little kids, and so of course we

would start cutting up and trying to make each other laugh, right? When we got out of line . . . my grandma would make us do that in a notebook. Whatever we did, we'd have to write it 100 times.

I Will Not Talk Back to My Grandma . . . I Will Not Talk Back to My Grandma . . . I Will Not Talk Back to My Grandma.

Chubb's grandmother also had him stand in front of the mirror and say, "I'm smart. I'm intelligent. I believe in myself."

She made him say that over and over . . . very clearly.

Chubb was a star at Cedartown High. His coach, Mike Worthington, was one of the most important people in his life. Worthington pushed Chubb hard. Chubb wanted to play for Georgia, and Worthington demanded that he work hard on his conditioning.

Chubb went to Georgia. He suffered a major knee injury in 2015. But he came back from the injury, and the Browns picked him in the second round of the 2018 draft.

When Browns general manager John Dorsey was looking at video of different college running backs in the 2018 draft, he sent video of Chubb to Jim Brown. The Browns great reviewed it and gave Chubb a rousing endorsement.

* * *

Jim Brown was 29 in his final season with the Browns. Chubb was 29 when the Browns elected not to offer him a contract for the 2025 season.

Chubb's career in Cleveland didn't match Jim Brown's career. Not even close. No one wearing a Browns helmet had a career like Jim Brown.

But when I think of Browns running backs, Jim Brown is No. 1.

And Chubb is No. 2.

Brown walked away from football in 1965. I am old enough to have watched him play. For those who aren't that old—or who

Fans hoping the Browns would bring back Nick Chubb for another year in 2025 were thinking with their hearts. The Browns were thinking of injuries and the salary cap. *Joshua Gunter / cleveland.com*

want to relive the memories of No. 32 carrying the football with one hand, just do a web search for "Jim Brown highlights."

Watch them and I'll let you come up with your own description.

Then search for video of highlights of Nick Chubb.

When watching those, there are moments when I think I'm watching Jim Brown.

The Browns have had other great running backs. Before Brown, there was Marion Motley (1946–53), also a Hall of Famer. I never saw Motley. After Brown was Leroy Kelly, another Hall of Famer.

I know that Brown admired Chubb as a player and a person.

Like Brown, Chubb never engaged in celebrations after scoring touchdowns. Go to the end zone, then calmly give the ball to the official. Brown's motto was: Act like you've been there before.

In terms of stats, Chubb ranks No. 3 on the team's all-time rushing list: Jim Brown (12,312 yards), Kelly (7,274 yards) and Chubb (6,843 yards).

The only other Cleveland running back with more than 5,500 career yards is Mike Pruitt (6,540).

Jim Brown averaged 5.2 yards per carry, behind Marion Motley's 5.7 yards. Then there's Chubb at 5.1 yards. No one else on the list of the Browns top 10 rushers averaged more than 5 yards per carry.

Like many fans, I was hoping the Browns would bring back Chubb for another year. But also like many fans, I was thinking with my heart.

Chubb was still battling back from the gruesome knee injury he suffered Sept. 18, 2023. During a Monday night loss to Pittsburgh, Chubb was hit near the goal line by defensive back Minkah Fitzpatrick. His knee bent back and off to the side.

Chubb suffered torn ACL and MCL ligaments along with other damage. The damage was so significant, he needed two surgeries within a three-month period to put his knee back together. Making it worse for Chubb, it was the same knee that had major reconstruction surgery when he was a running back at Georgia in 2015. Chubb returned to the Browns 13 months after the injury. It was remarkable that he made it back that soon. Perhaps he came back too soon, but Chubb had to believe he was fighting for his career.

Chubb was back on the field Oct. 20, 2024. That was 398 days from that awful night in Pittsburgh. He played eight games, carried the ball 102 times. He averaged only 3.2 yards per attempt.

Chubb was still a warrior. His blocking on blitzing linebackers was fierce and effective. He threw his body into tacklers for tough short yardage again. But the speed and the sharp cut that made Nick Chubb great were gone. Then Chubb's season ended when he suffered a broken foot Dec. 15, 2024, in a loss to Kansas City.

* * *

At the Browns training camp in 2023 in Greenbrier, West Virginia, Chubb talked about how the NFL was devaluing running backs. To some extent, all football players are considered replaceable parts. But in the age of analytics, most teams believe it would be wiser to draft a running back on a rookie contract than pay a veteran.

"Next year it could be me in the same situation," said Chubb. "I understand the situation. I know it can be me one day."

That's exactly what happened as the Browns drafted two running backs in 2025: Ohio State's Quinshon Judkins and Tennessee's Dylan Sampson.

The Browns knew more about Chubb's medical situation because he'd been with them since 2018. They also were watching every penny on their salary cap because they were still dealing with the consequences of the monster Deshaun Watson contract. My sense is the Browns didn't want to bring Chubb to camp and cut him.

Chubb will always be missed by many Browns fans, including me.

* * *

Why did Jim Brown leave the Browns at the age of 29?

When I was researching the 1964 Browns, several players told me how they resented owner Art Modell's decision to not be patient with Jim Brown. Brown had started a second career as an actor. He was making the movie *The Dirty Dozen* and would miss training camp before the 1966 season. This bothered Modell. It became a test of wills.

Brown's last season was 1965. He rushed for an NFL-best 1,544 yards and 17 TDs.

"I told Art that I was leaving, but if he needed me, I might consider coming back," Brown told me in an interview for *Browns Town 1964*. "The movie was taking longer to finish than they thought. Art was putting out all these statements about how he had to fine me if

I didn't show up in camp. I told Art, 'Hey, you have a one-way contract, I only get paid if I play. I'm not guaranteed any money.' How could he fine me when I wasn't even being paid?"

Brown then decided he'd had enough of football—or at least, of Modell. He gave the story of his retirement to Plain Dealer sports editor Hal Lebovitz, whom he was very close with. And with that, he walked away from football.

A statue of Jim Brown stands outside of Browns Stadium. Some fans still wear No. 32 Jim Brown jerseys to games. Some of them are not old enough to have watched Brown play, but they embrace the legend, the history.

FANS WRITE IN ABOUT NICK CHUB . . .

My favorite quote about Nick Chubb came from Kevin Stefanski. When asked which Brown he'd have no problem babysitting his kids, he instantly answered Nick Chubb. Stefanski then said he'd let Chubb do his taxes.

— Ron Pruchnicki

In a league filled with showboating and "promoting your own brand," whatever that means, I never once saw Chubb even point to signal a first down let alone do a touchdown dance. You never saw him indulging in nightlife or being a distraction in any way, whether that was off the field or handling his interactions with the media. . . . It's one thing to be quiet while you are sitting on the bench, it's another to be producing at an all-time level and still have Chubb's humility. His game on the field had a bit of everything, from the breakaway speed, to the nasty stiff arm, to the elusive change of direction, and the elite vision. . . . To sum it up, Nick Chubb: hero, warrior, role model, Cleveland Brown for life.

— Tyler Lance, Algona, Iowa

I am sad Nick Chubb is gone. Equally sad that I purchased a signed Nick Chubb real Browns jersey for $150 for my grandson.

— Bruce Garlitz, Westlake, Ohio

In an era where great Cleveland draft picks have been as rare as a Honus Wagner baseball card, the Nick Chubb pick meant everything. He was what was right about Cleveland.

— Michael Reihard, Leavittsburg, Ohio

Nick Chubb is, by far, my favorite Cleveland Browns player since 1999. He exemplifies everything a fan could ask for . . . a humble, hard-working superstar who embodies Cleveland work ethic.

— Bob McLean, Delafield, Wisconsin

The first time Nick Chubb handed the ball to the referee after a touchdown, he was my favorite Brown.

— Tom Yochim, Erie, Pennsylvania

JIM DONOVAN'S LONG BATTLE WITH CANCER

It didn't start out like cancer. No clue it was cancer. No strange bumps, nothing much out of the ordinary.

Jim Donovan, the longtime radio voice of the Browns, talked with me about his health and his battle with cancer for different newspaper stories over the years. The last time we spoke was a few months before his death on Oct. 26, 2024.

"It was during training camp in 2000," he said. "I just didn't feel that good, pretty tired. I went to one of those 24-hour walk-in places. They ran a blood test."

As Donovan awaited the results, he thought about how he rarely was sick. He was 43 years old. Probably nothing to worry about—even after he'd sat there for more than 30 minutes.

"We're going to take the blood test again," the doctor said. Donovan still wasn't that concerned.

After the second test, they told him, "You have a very elevated white blood cell count. You either have an infection, or you're showing signs you have leukemia."

Donovan felt his heart sink. His legs "turned to rubber." He kept thinking . . . *leukemia . . . how can it be leukemia?* He didn't feel very sick, except for an upset stomach. And whose stomach wouldn't be churning after hearing that news?

His next stop was his family doctor, more blood tests, more of the same results—white blood cells numbers going up. He was diagnosed with chronic lymphocytic leukemia (CLL).

"An alarm went off in my head," said Donovan. "My dad had that. He was very understated about it. I remembered him saying, 'I have this thing called CLL.' "

That conversation happened after Donovan had just done his first national NFL game for NBC. That was in 1987.

"I'm sorry, I didn't see the game," Jim Donovan Sr. told his son. "I was in the hospital. My mouth sort of blew up. But I'm OK. I'm not going to die from it."

Then Donovan remembered that his uncle had also had CLL.

Now he had it.

Donovan's father was right. He didn't die from CLL. But he later developed pancreatic cancer and died at the age of 63. Donovan was very aware of how a family medical history can be passed down from one generation to the next.

"I became neurotic about my blood count," said Donovan. "I kept waiting for it to go down. I kept thinking it was a mistake because I didn't feel any different."

But the numbers didn't lie. Something was very wrong. After about two years, his doctors began treating it with chemotherapy.

"The first sessions were bad," he said. "They hooked me up to an IV for one week a month—five days. And that went on for six months. It worked right away. I went into remission and it lasted three years."

For years, Donovan only told his family and a few people close to him about his condition.

"Around 2005, it [leukemia] came back," said Donovan. "It was more aggressive. The leukemia got smart to the old drugs, and they had to use new drugs. This time, I got really sick. I went into about 75% remission. It didn't last long."

His Browns radio partner and close friend Doug Dieken knew about Donovan's medical condition.

"He'd tell you he was getting some treatments," said Dieken. "But it wasn't complaining. Only thing he'd say was, 'I'm really tired today.' Jimmy was a warrior, a very positive guy."

During the various chemotherapy treatments, Donovan was being told he'd eventually need a bone marrow transplant.

"I was dead set against it," he said. "They talked about me being in the hospital for something like six months. I'd be away from work. It was overwhelming. I kept wanting to treat it the way we'd been doing."

In 2008, Donovan's condition became more dire. Lots of fatigue and other problems from the CLL.

"I was off (from WKYC) for most of the summer," he said. "Nothing was said publicly. I came back in time for the Browns' preseason games."

He also was being told he would soon need a bone marrow transplant.

"I kept putting it off," he said. "I was taking chemo, they tried different drugs. But it wasn't working."

* * *

Near the end of the 2009 season, the Browns had a game in Kansas City.

"I was doing the Browns' sideline reporting back then," said Andre Knott, now a member of the Cleveland Guardians TV broadcast team. "Jimmy had something like a 103-degree fever that night [before the game]. He was in terrible shape."

Knott was told to be ready to pinch hit for Donovan the next morning.

"The night before the game, Doug [Dieken] went and got one of the team doctors to come to my room," said Donovan. "I was really sick and had a fever. The doctor said he'd watch me. The next morning, I felt awful as I went up to the booth in Kansas City."

Donovan doubted he'd be able to broadcast the game. He expressed his concerns to Dieken.

"You're probably going to get a jolt of adrenaline," said Dieken, the former star left tackle for the Browns. "You'll be fine during the game. But after that . . . look out."

Dieken was right. Donovan broadcast one of the best games of the season, with the Browns beating Kansas City, 41-34. Josh Cribbs had remarkable kickoff returns of 100 and 103 yards for touchdowns. Jerome Harrison carried the ball 34 times for 286 yards and three touchdowns.

Donovan was so absorbed with the game, the pain and fatigue went away. For three hours, he felt wonderful.

"On the team plane going home, it was like Christmas," said Donovan. "Everybody was so happy. But I crashed. I got home and then went to the doctor's. I knew at that point, I was going to have to get the transplant."

Knott said many on the flight to Cleveland knew Donovan was very sick.

"Jimmy is a nervous flier," said Knott. "You'd never know it because he likes to talk to people, tell stories, walk around on those chartered flights. It's his way of dealing with flying. But that night, he just sat there."

There was no choice. Donovan realized he needed a bone marrow transplant or he was likely to die. Donovan learned they put a sample of your blood on a world bank looking for a donor match. It would be year—the spring of 2011—until a donor was found.

"There were two," said Donovan. "One in this country, one in Germany. Both perfect, 10 out of 10. They did the one in this country. They don't tell you who is the donor. They admit you to the hospital. They bombard you with chemotherapy until your immune system is all the way down to zero. It's lethal stuff."

Donovan recalled all the nurses and doctors in masks and gowns.

"There was a whiteboard in the room and they kept track of how it was going until I was ready," Donovan said. "I was there about 10 days before the transfusion. The donor gave it in Nashville. Then they brought in the marrow transplant in a bag, and they gave it to me with an IV."

The transfusion itself was a success.

"But that night, I ran a high fever . . . 104," said Donovan. "It went on for three days. I was having hallucinations. I remember telling a nurse I thought I'd die."

The nurse told Donovan: "Don't say that. We'll figure it out."

They did figure it out. One of the antibiotics had triggered a reaction. The medication was changed.

Donovan's transplant was June 7, 2011. His goal was to call the first Browns game—Sept. 11, 2011.

As for the donor, all Donovan knew was that there was a 33-year-old male out there . . . somewhere. He didn't know his name or where he lived, just somewhere in the United States. He didn't donate it for anyone in particular, just for someone who needed it.

"If he hadn't donated, who knows where I'd be," Donovan told me about a year after the transfusion.

Eventually, the Donovans learned the donor's identity, and added a new member to the family— Dallas Gentry, a corrections officer from Wise, Virginia.

"After a year, you can say you'd like to meet or correspond with the donor," said Donovan. "The donor doesn't have to do it. But he did. Dallas came for Thanksgiving (in 2012) and it was unbelievable. We had the greatest holiday you could ever have."

Gentry visited the Donovans several times over the years. They also went to his home in rural Virginia.

"You could have made a Hallmark movie out of it," said Donovan. "I am so grateful to all the people who have been with me through all this."

* * *

Donovan learned during his battle with cancer that it never really goes away. Even when it is "gone" and you're in remission, it's still there. You think about it. You have to wait for the next tests and scans.

"When you come home after the transfusion, you go see doctors about three times a week for all kinds of testing," said Donovan. "That included a dermatologist. I had this patch on my earlobe. They tested it and it was melanoma. I was in a bad spot because I had no immune system."

The news was shocking. After all he'd been through, now a mole on the earlobe? A bad mole? Really?

Many who have had a serious bout with cancer can tell you this: There are times when the physical pain is matched by the emotional strain of more bad news. That was how Donovan felt a few weeks before the 2011 season when the earlobe became an issue.

"They did the surgery to remove the mole," he said. "They were worried about it [the melanoma] spreading. If it spread, it would ruin the transplant. We were devastated. We thought we had been through the transplant and everything else—now the mole came up."

Then came the waiting. Donovan recalled a night sitting on his porch. All was quiet, except his thoughts. After all he had been through, he suddenly feared it was a mole . . . on his earlobe . . . that was going to kill him.

"We had to sweat it out for a week before the pathology report (on the mole) came back," said Donovan. "It didn't spread. I did the Browns' opener. I missed one game in San Francisco. I got pneumonia. You're very vulnerable to that after the transplant."

Knott remembers all of this as "a scary time. Jimmy was getting hit with one thing after another. But he said very little about it. Jimmy is an incredible guy."

"I played in the NFL for 14 years and never missed a game," said

A tribute to the late Jim Donovan—"Voice of the Cleveland Browns"—before a game in October 2024. "Jimmy lived to do the games," said longtime broadcast partner Doug Dieken. *Joshua Gunter / cleveland.com*

Dieken. "I played with a lot of tough guys. But the toughest guys are not always on the field."

Earlier in his broadcast career, Dieken had been paired up with Nev Chandler when the Browns' play-by-play man (1985–93) was struck with colon cancer. Chandler died Aug. 7, 1994, at the age of 47.

"Jimmy and Nev are the two toughest guys I've ever been around," said Dieken. "Nev and Jimmy would come into the booth. They had been drained all week by cancer treatments, and they'd still crank up the energy."

He saw many similarities between the two.

"They both brought so much enthusiasm to the game," said Dieken. "I'd sit there like a bump on a log and I'd get my energy from their energy. I'd want guys like that on my team any day."

* * *

Donovan took joy in hearing from people who walked the same road.

"There are times when I can help people going through it," he said. "I didn't know a lot about leukemia when I got it—or about the transplant. Now, I've been there. For example, the 100-day mark is a huge milestone. People write to me to say they got to 100 days . . . or the one-year mark. We can celebrate together."

Over the decades, Donovan received a thousand . . . probably more than that . . . cards and letters.

"I received holy relics from nuns," he said. "I kept thinking about all the love from so many people in Cleveland . . . and I'm not even from here."

Donovan's wife, Cheryl, and his daughter, Meghan, were a team during the ordeal. They went through treatments, the setbacks, side effects, doubts and the flat-out frightening times.

"I met Cheryl at the old Arcade in downtown Cleveland," said Donovan. "She worked at a barber shop on the third floor. My best friend, Jim Hooley [at WKYC], was a stickler about his TV hair, and she used to cut his hair."

This was in 1988 when Donovan was a 32-year-old sportscaster. Hooley and Donovan needed green ties for a St. Patrick's Day show and planned to shop together.

"Hooley said to meet him at the old Arcade staircase," said Donovan. "He said if he wasn't there, he'd be at the barber shop on the third floor. That's where I found him. Cheryl was cutting his hair. We met in 1988 that day, and got married in 1989."

The wedding was 11 years before the first leukemia diagnosis.

Early in their marriage, the Donovans lived in Westlake. Cheryl loves horses. Same with Meghan, who works in the University of Akron sports information department. They spent a lot of time at the stable, caring for and riding horses. Finally, they decided to buy a place where they could live and keep the horses.

"Cheryl took me to this 12-acre hay field," said Donovan. "We rode around in a golf cart. She was talking about building a home, a barn. . . . I didn't get it and told her that. I grew up in Boston playing street hockey. She looked at me and said, 'I get it.' She designed this place, and it's beautiful."

Donovan helped take care of the horses. They owned two and boarded a third at the barn. The place is tranquil, green hills and with chirping birds supplying the backdrop.

"Cheryl has been a rock through all of this," said Donovan. "When it happens to you, you're stunned. You just don't know what to think or say. You need someone in the room with you to ask questions, to listen . . . and to be your advocate."

Donovan's voice cracked as he talked about his wife and daughter.

"Sometimes, you need someone to fight for you," he said, "When you go through something like this, your voice isn't as strong as it is on a fall Sunday afternoon at the Browns' game. Plus, she had to take care of everything at home."

* * *

On the day after Jimmy Donovan died (Oct. 26, 2024), I called Doug Dieken. For 23 years, Doug Dieken and Donovan had done Browns games together on radio. That ended when Dieken retired after the 2021 season.

But they shared one last game together. It was at Donovan's home on Oct. 6, 2024. The two men sat in front of the TV set, both realizing it would be special. Donovan had stepped away from the radio booth a few weeks before the 2024 season opened. Dieken had talked to Donovan several times since that game. He visited Donovan in hospice a few times.

"He knew," said Dieken.

The former Browns offensive lineman's voice cracked.

"You never know when it's going to be the last rodeo," he said. "We were just two guys watching a Browns game."

Final score: Washington 34, Browns 13.

Over the years, they called so many games just like that together.

Really bad football. Dieken laughed as he recalled that, saying how the two buddies talked about the game like they sometimes had wished they could while watching the Browns' incompetence from the radio booth.

"No way you could put that on the radio," he laughed. "It was strictly cable TV, if you know what I mean. It was a lot of 'Oh, crap . . . what was that?' We told some stories I can't tell you [for the public]. He was typical Jimmy . . . upbeat . . . He never wanted anyone to feel sorry for him."

Andre Knott had a long conversation with Donovan on Sept. 5, 2024.

"That was the date they announced Andrew [Siciliano] would replace Jimmy on the radio (for the 2024 season)," said Knott. "Jimmy had told the Browns he couldn't do the games because of his health. But I knew it would be tough for him when the news came out. He liked Andrew, but it still hurt."

To Donovan, it felt like the final door was shutting.

"Jimmy lived to do the games," Dieken said.

Donovan had spent 39 years at WKYC as a sports and news anchor. He also did some network TV for the NFL before becoming the voice of the Browns. Despite all the TV experience, he was a radio man at heart. Former Cavs broadcaster Joe Tait told me that about Donovan—the highest praise.

Knott said, "Jimmy was so important to me early in my career. He told me stuff to make me better. When I was let go by the Browns, Jimmy called and said something better was coming, don't give up."

That turned out to be true. Knott was hired to do Cleveland's baseball games on television, a job he's had for the last 12 years

"In my last conversation with Jimmy, I became very emotional. I told him I'm able to do what I'm doing now because of what I learned from him."

Dieken found himself talking about the special relationship

radio play-by-play voices have with the listeners. He mentioned former Cavs radio voice Joe Tait, Donovan and longtime Guardians radio voice Tom Hamilton.

"Those three are on the Mount Rushmore [of broadcasters]," he said. "Too bad our teams here haven't been as good as those guys were on the radio."

* * *

Not long after Donovan died, I received this email from reader Tim Huhta:

> Our 20-year-old son was diagnosed with cancer and faced three months of chemo. I've been a Browns season ticket holder since 1995. I reached out to Jimmy, telling him what my son was facing—and we are at every game. Maybe I thought he would send him a letter? A card. Jim called Logan on his way to Cincinnati last year, saying he was thinking of Logan and wanted to check in. He called him the morning of the game. They would text and talk on the phone many times over Logan's three-month ordeal.
>
> Even as Jimmy faced his awful news, Logan and Jimmy continued to text and encourage each other. I feel like we lost a great friend. Jimmy didn't have to do what he did for my son. My family will never forget the time he took to help Logan fight his fight.

QUARTERBACKS. AGAIN.

Back when the new Browns expansion franchise was preparing for its first season in 1999, the team was looking for a quarterback.

"You always want to begin a new team with a quarterback," said Carmen Policy, the team's CEO at the time.

And 25 years later?

The Browns were still looking.

Tim Couch was the first draft selection of the new Browns in 1999. He wasn't the first quarterback to play in a regular season game. That was Ty Detmer. A former 1990 Heisman Trophy winner, Detmer was 31 when he took the field for that first game. He had been mostly a career backup.

By the fourth quarter of a 43-0 opening day loss to Pittsburgh at Browns Stadium, Detmer had already been replaced by Couch.

Those were quarterbacks No. 1 and No. 2 in a generally dismal parade of 40 different men trying to play the position from 1999 to 2024.

Compare that with the Baltimore Ravens (the old Browns). In 2008 they settled on Joe Flacco as their starting quarterback. In the middle of the 2018 season, they handed the job over to Lamar Jackson, who still holds the job as of this writing, seven years later.

From 2008 to 2025, Baltimore was set with Flacco and Jackson.

In that 18-year span, only 19 total games were not started by Flacco or Jackson. That's right, 19 in 18 years. Flacco started 163 games out of a possible 169 before he was benched in favor of Jackson. The six he missed in that period were due to injuries. Jackson missed a few games here and there due to injuries.

Meanwhile, the Browns . . .

The Lerner family (Al, then Randy) owned the team from 1999 to 2012. They had a combined record of 69-146 (.321) and one playoff appearance. The Haslam family officially became owners Oct. 25, 2012. From that point through 2024, they had a record of 72-132-1 (.351) with two playoff appearances.

In that span from 1999 to 2024, of the Browns' 40—40!—starting quarterbacks, only four have won at least 10 games:

Baker Mayfield: 29-30.

Tim Couch: 22-37.

Derek Anderson: 16-18.

Brian Hoyer: 10-6.

Here's a list of the Browns' Week 1 quarterbacks since 1999:

1999: Ty Detmer
2000: Tim Couch
2001: Tim Couch
2002: Kelly Holcomb
2003: Kelly Holcomb
2004: Jeff Garcia
2005: Trent Dilfer
2006: Charlie Frye
2007: Derek Anderson
2008: Derek Anderson
2009: Brady Quinn
2010: Jake Delhomme
2011: Colt McCoy
2012: Brandon Weeden

2013: Brandon Weeden
2014: Brian Hoyer
2015: Johnny Manziel
2016: Robert Griffin III
2017: DeShone Kizer
2018: Tyrod Taylor
2019: Baker Mayfield
2020: Baker Mayfield
2021: Baker Mayfield
2022: Jacoby Brissett
2023: Deshaun Watson
2024: Deshaun Watson

There you have it: The Browns had 19 different Week 1 starting quarterbacks.

They also had 20 different offensive coordinators.

All in 25 years since the franchise returned.

Heading into their 26th season, the Browns needed . . .

You got it, a quarterback.

They entered training camp in 2025 not having picked a starting quarterback. In fact, the guys who had played the position in 2024 were all gone at the start of camp: Jameis Winston, Dorian Thompson-Robinson, Bailey Zappe and Deshaun Watson. At the end of camp, Zappe was brought back for depth and Watson was placed on the physically unable to perform list.

Watson was still on their 2025 roster, but he was out of the plans as he was recovering from his second Achilles surgery. Even if Watson had stayed healthy, the Browns were going to bring in other quarterbacks to truly compete with him for the job.

After a dismal 3-14 season in 2024, the Browns looked at their quarterbacks like a bad hand of cards. They decided to throw them all on the table and ask the dealer for all new cards—except for Watson. They had to keep that card, but not play it. The elephan-

Joe Flacco—even at 39 years old—looked the part of an NFL quarterback. Still, the onetime Super Bowl MVP arrived in Cleveland as an underdog.
John Kuntz / cleveland.com

tine impact of Watson's contract on the salary cap required that he remain on the injured list.

Goodbye to the old.

Hello to Kenny Pickett (temporarily, before he was traded to the Las Vegas Raiders), Shedeur Sanders, Dillon Gabriel and Joe Flacco.

Joe Flacco . . .

He earned a special place in the hearts of many Browns fans with his performance in the 2023 season. (The 2023 Browns are probably my favorite team since the franchise returned in 1999.)

That season was a Kevin Stefanski masterpiece of coaching.

The Browns opened the 2023 season with Deshaun Watson at quarterback. He suffered a shoulder injury requiring major surgery Nov. 21, 2023. That came in a 33-31 victory over Baltimore. He already had been dealing with a sore shoulder that cost him four starts.

Although he was credited with only one victory after being claimed on waivers by the Browns, P.J. Walker really won two games. He replaced Watson late in the first quarter of a game in Indianapolis and helped the Browns beat the Colts.

Dorian Thompson-Robinson beat the Steelers.

But it was Joe Flacco who truly came to the rescue. Flacco arrived in Cleveland with a career 18-3 record against the Browns, most of it as a member of the dreaded Ravens. He had been written off after the 2022 season. He could not even secure an invitation to try out in a training camp in 2023.

It was Flacco whom a desperate GM Andrew Berry called in the middle of November to fly to Cleveland for a midweek tryout. No promises. He worked out with a bunch of other guys who were begging for even a spot on the practice squad.

In his 11 seasons with the Ravens, Flacco had a 96-67 record as a starter. He was a Super Bowl MVP in 2012. Only twice did he have a losing season. His playoff record was 10-5. While he bounced from Baltimore to Denver to New York after being dumped by the Ravens after the 2018 season, he still arrived at the Browns training facility in 2023 as a man worthy of respect. The orange helmets knew what he had done to them over more than a decade.

Once Flacco began to throw the ball, the Browns knew his arm was still strong. Very strong. The strongest arm of any Browns quarterback since 1999. He also had confidence and a quick ability to learn an offense.

At 6-foot-6 and 230 pounds, Flacco—even at 39 years old—looked the part of an NFL quarterback. Although he told the media he "got off my couch" to come to Cleveland, he actually had been getting up at 6 a.m. to work out five days a week. He threw passes to friends. He remained in tremendous shape as he awaited a call.

Now, he played the part of the old sheriff coming into a town that needed someone to simply say, "I'm in charge" without needing to speak the words.

This was a classic underdog story, the rejected Raven coming to Cleveland . . . and winning games for the orange helmets.

Browns fans watched Flacco throw the ball downfield—as though flipped with no effort yet zipping 40 yards.

Veteran receiver Amari Cooper called Flacco "a faith multiplier." Was that a knock on Watson and the other quarterbacks? You decide.

"When Flacco showed up, it brought back the excitement and reminded me of my teenage years and Bernie Kosar," reader Kent Conklin emailed me.

"Joe Flacco was a breath of fresh air," wrote another fan, Dale DeRemer. "He seemed to pull the team together and was fun to watch."

Flacco was 4-1 as a starter for the Browns. Always prone to interceptions, he thew eight of them in those five games. But he also fired 13 TD passes. He averaged 321 yards passing per game.

Browns fan Jay Casey became so excited, he created a song called "Flacco" to the tune of "Lola" by the Kinks. (There also was a song like that called "Bernie, Bernie" about Bernie Kosar in the late 1980s.)

Flacco would go to a Dunkin' Donuts in a West Side Cleveland suburb to pick up breakfast on the way to the Browns' practice facility during the week. Fans kept sending me pictures of themselves with Flacco at Dunkin' Donuts. Fans sent those pictures everywhere.

Joe Flacco—the everyman—at Dunkin' Donuts. He may have been a Raven for 11 years, but he's a Cleveland kind of guy.

"Once Joe Flacco started winning games here, I no longer cared that he used to play for the Ravens," emailed fan Brian DiTullio.

It all came to an end when the Browns went to Houston for a playoff game. The Texans hammered the Browns, 45-14. Flacco threw back-to-back interceptions in the third quarter that were run back for touchdowns by Houston.

That 2023 season ended, but I had so much fun writing about it—especially the Flacco period.

"I went to the playoff game in Houston with my wife," emailed Matt Barnes. "Although it didn't turn out how we hoped (and some Texans fans threw beer at us), I enjoyed the season. I don't take years like that for granted."

I felt the same way.

But in true Browns fashion, the team didn't bring back Flacco in 2024. Why? They said (on background) that they wanted a younger quarterback. Jameis Winston was 30 when they signed him, nine years younger than Flacco. But the real reason was that they were re-designing the offense, with new offensive coaches, to accommodate Watson. The Browns also knew if Watson struggled early, many fans and media members would be demanding that Flacco play. They worried about Watson's confidence, especially coming off major shoulder surgery.

Naturally, almost none of that plan went right in 2024.

WHY THE BROWNS?

Ever ask yourself, *Why the Browns?*

Why do fans stick with this team?

Why not follow the Packers . . . the Chiefs . . .

I started to write, "even the Steelers," but I know the answer to that question. Hard to believe anyone from Cleveland would root for the Pittsburgh Steelers.

My friend Mary Kelly refuses to wear black and gold, the Steelers' colors. Along with my wife, Roberta, Mary is a member of the choir at Akron's Arlington Church of God. The choir director designates certain colors to be worn on Sundays when the choir sings. When Dr. Leslie Parker Barnes says it's time for black and gold—or even black and yellow—Mary refuses, and will wear only black.

Once, Roberta showed up at church wearing a yellow raincoat and black slacks. Mary erupted, "How can you wear THOSE COLORS?"

"Mary, it's a raincoat," said Roberta.

Mary wasn't placated. Steeler colors are Steeler colors, and no Browns fan should wear them for any reason—even protection from the rain.

Browns fans . . . You can't make this kind of story up.

"I have Browns lamps, T-shirts, blankets, jackets, pillows and jewelry," Mary said. "I even had a Browns ceramic Christmas tree that is out all year. My mom surprised me with the gift and I think of her every time I see it."

Mary also has orange and brown elephant hats and lots of Browns autographs. She was shaken when the Browns acquired Deshaun Watson with all his off-field baggage, but not enough to swear off the Browns.

What makes Browns fans like this?

Why do Browns fans stick with a team that has disappointed them over and over and over again since 1999?

I posed that question to readers of my newsletter on social media.

Among the many responses was this from JoAnne deHamel:

> The Browns have made me proud, extremely anxious, mad, sad and sick. My husband is from Scotland. He became a Browns fan when he moved here in 1988. He recently passed away and he wrote 'GO BROWNS' on a piece of paper . . . as he lay on his deathbed!

I read that and just started laughing. No insult intended, but don't tell me that following the Browns is logical.

JoAnne continued:

> I'm just praying that I will see the Browns win a Super Bowl before I die. If I don't, I will always be a crazy fan . . . I've been watching them since 1952 . . . when I was 2 years old. That's a test of fortitude, if you ask me.

I won't bother to ask how she watched the Browns at the age of 2. Her parents did have season tickets, so she was probably still in diapers while going to games in the 1950s when the great Paul Brown coached championship teams.

Consider this email from Steve Edelman:

Is this young fan bragging or seeking pity? Even though they know it brings heartache, Browns fans continue to pass down the tradition.
David Petkiewicz / cleveland.com

I was 9 years old when the Browns won their last championship in 1964. I was aware of football, but it didn't do anything for me. The day of the 1964 championship game against Baltimore, my mom had taken my brother and me to see a movie. When we got home, the game had just ended. My dad had listened to it on the radio. The postgame show with Gib Shanley and Jim Graner was on.

My dad was a concentration camp survivor. He was blinded in the Nazi camp and came to the U.S. with my mom in 1951. He had never seen a football (or baseball) game but somehow figured out what was going on and developed a real liking for the two sports. Maybe it was the soothing voices of the Gibber (Gib Shanley) and Jimmy Dudley. He was a man of little emotion. But when we came into the house after the movie, he had a big smile on his face. He told me what had happened and I was enthralled. I couldn't wait for the Plain Dealer to arrive the next morning so I could devour

> the sports page and read all about the game. I was hooked. I couldn't wait for the 1965 season so I could listen to the games on radio with my dad, and the rest is history . . . Gib, Nev, Casey and Jimmy ARE the Cleveland Browns to me. Players, coaches, front office people and owners are here for a second. Those broadcasters are the constant that define Cleveland football for me.

Being a Browns fan is about more than the Browns. It's about family and heart. And yes, loyalty. It's the family connection that interests me the most.

Susan Frollo wrote:

> I became a Browns fan purely by accident back in the 1960s. When I was 'grounded,' I was forced to sit in the living room and watch football with my dad. It was bad enough that I couldn't go outside or play in my room—my dad insisted I pay attention to the game as he explained it to me. Over time, I learned the positions, the plays, the players, and the strategies and came to enjoy watching the games. I fantasized about being the first female sportscaster.

As I read through the many emails I received and saw how your hearts show through in your stories, I realized that was the main reason to write this book.

So, again . . . Why the Browns?

Maybe because the Browns are as much about you as about the team on the field and the staff in the front office and the owners.

Why not let fans answer that question?

Here's what you had to say . . .

FANS WRITE IN: WHY I STILL FOLLOW THE BROWNS . . .

What keeps me watching the Browns? I remember watching the World Series when the Boston Red Sox and then the Chicago Cubs finally got over the hump and won it all. Old men were sitting in the stands crying their eyes out. Sitting, crying and celebrating, in the same seats where they practically grew up watching their favorite teams as children with their parents. I imagine them replaying all those years of frustration and futility to that moment. No more waiting until next year. This was their year. I WANT THAT. I want that soul purging cry. I want to say the football team passed down to me from my father and from me to my sons, my favorite team, are the World Champions. The best. It would make all of the jokes and teasing and 0-16, and the Drive, the Fumble, the Move, Art Modell's ineptitude—all of the years of being a laughing stock would be gone. I would be able to cry and think about all of it and my faith would finally be rewarded.

— Clarence D. Meriweather, Akron, Ohio

The pain of following the Browns, I have become convinced, is a feature, not a bug. Look, all of us have been hurt at one time or another—by spouses, coworkers, friends, siblings. When that happens, our choice is pretty clear—we can either move on from them or accept that they are humans with flaws, forgive them and love them for the good in them. And if we can't do that, what are we even doing on this earth?

— Greg Thomas, Hudson, Ohio

Dealing with the pain is part of what makes Cleveland fans the best around. The loyalty, the perseverance, the resourcefulness, the ability to laugh while crying, the camaraderie that comes with one common goal of just friggin' winning one — lol! OK maybe the camaraderie is more of a trauma bond, but still I love my city, I love my Browns, and I love that I'm not alone in this, because what happens during Cleveland games, well ya just can't make this up. Tip of the day: work out on a punching/kicking bag during halftime so you're too tired to be upset in the second half.

— Elke Sündermann, Cleveland, Ohio

I was lucky enough to grow up with my dad having season tickets in the Dawg Pound. The folks that sat around me watched me grow up. The hug I would give to the woman who sat next to me the first time I saw her each year was a highlight of every season. "Collective effervescence" is the technical, psychological term for the feeling evoked when you're surrounded by 70,000 others all screaming and chanting for the same thing.

For better or for worse, following the Browns is a fundamental part of who I am. Could I try to beat that out of myself? Sure. But for what? So I no longer have something that keeps me connected to loved ones that live in different states? So I'm less annoyed 12-16 Sundays a year? I guess that'd be fine. But what's greater: the annoyance veering into anger I feel when watching this franchise operate, or the joy I derive from seeing it succeed, and sharing that joy with friends and family? I'll take the latter, eight days a week.

— Aaron Corpora, Philadelphia, Pennsylvania

I continue to watch the Browns for two reasons: Carrying on tradition and optimism. My grandfather and my great-uncle were big Browns fans, and every Sunday my great-uncle would come over to watch the game with my grandparents. This went on for as long as I can remember. Both passed away in recent years, but watching the Browns helps me feel that connection. It takes me back to them yelling at the TV screen. Sometimes it was excitement. Sometimes it was disappointment. Regardless, they tuned in and hoped the Browns came away with the win.

— Davion Moore, Sandusky, Ohio

Joshua Gunter / The Plain Dealer

I have gone from a true fanatic—all three AFC championship games, family season tickets since 1986, a flag used to hang from the front of my house . . . Now, I really don't watch anymore but keep a passive eye on it as if I cannot give it up totally. I am just tired of the stupidness of the team from top to bottom. I am REALLY sorry I passed this on to my four sons.

— Jim McCarthy, Strongsville, Ohio

What keeps me watching the Browns is the long history of the team. My parents divorced when I was 7 and Sundays were days with my dad. He would make chili and we would watch the Browns and he taught me about the rules, the plays and the great players in the '60s and '70s . My favorite was Leroy Kelly! My dad is gone now but every Sunday when I make my batch of chili, my family and I cheer on the Browns during the highs and lows of each season. I'll always have that memory of Sundays with my dad and him singing "Go Brownies!"

— Laura Alvarez, Round Rock, Texas

I still follow the Browns despite not planning to watch this year. I can't change teams. I have too many memories and experiences from the Kardiac Kids and Bernie eras. I just now refuse to become

Joshua Gunter / cleveland.com

emotionally invested in the Browns. I expect the worst and those expectations are sadly almost always met.

— Matt Pencek, Milton, Delaware

I still follow the Browns because it has been engrained in me since I was 6 years old (at the start of the 1999 season, with Tim Couch leading the new look Browns). Every Sunday watching games with my dad, getting season tickets of my own when I was 21, and continuing to live the tradition every year. I now have a 2-year-old son of my own. Taking him to training camp last year for the first time brought me to tears of joy, and I look forward to taking him to his first preseason game in August. The challenges and heart breaks will pay off when the good times arrive.

— Danny Poutz, Brunswick, Ohio

I was sitting in the stands with my brother during a 2013 game against Jacksonville in which the Browns were playing their typical miserable game—against a bad team. I turned to my brother and said "I don't know why I come to these games." The next play, Josh Gordon scored on a 95-yard TD. Amid the celebration, I turned to my brother and said, "That's why!" For me, it's about family, tradition . . . and hope.

— Bob Heintel, Monroe, North Carolina

I watch the Browns because they're my home. They're memories of my dad and mom making snacks and gathering around the TV. They're memories of my buddies and I in the backyard—"You're Derek Anderson, I'm Kellen Winslow, we're on the 45-yard line, 2nd-and-8. Run a fly route!" They remind me of what it means to be a little kid again. My dad has congestive heart failure, and I don't know if we'll get to watch a Browns game together this year. Even if we don't, I'll still go to my parents' home and make sure there's a Bud Light next to his chair. I'll always hear him yelling for Crennel to put in Brady Quinn. I'll always hold on to all the good and bad memories of the Browns because I shared them with my dad. He told me they might not always win, but just because they don't win doesn't mean they don't matter.

— Thomas Roth, Ashtabula, Ohio

I love the Browns, but I'm so tired of horrible drafts, bad decisions, undersized players and the meddlesome owner. I'll watch all the games, but without the emotional investment. Fandom addiction. It's part of me. I swore I was done after 3-14, but here I am, still absorbing all the Browns content I can. I see the orange helmets on the field in Berea for minicamp and I suffer a relapse.

— Dan Feiwell, Solon, Ohio

Why do I continue to follow a team that is often less entertaining than a late-night infomercial? If you had asked me before April 1, 2025, I would have told you I watched out of a loyalty to the team or to my dad, who was 21 the last time the Browns last won a title. But all that changed when my brother, a longtime Browns season ticket holder and my best friend in the world, lost his fight with leukemia this year. I now follow this team just to keep that connection with my brother alive. I'll watch and follow this team, our team, for him. The Haslams may technically own the Browns but it belongs to all of us seeking a personal escape or a connection to family and community. We watch the good, the bad and the awful, because we have to. It's who we are.

— Eric Furniss, Marion, Ohio

My mom was a huge Browns fan. She grew up when they were champions. We had a Browns pennant on our wall for as long as I could remember. My mom's twin sister was a Steelers fan. Not sure what that was about. Well, back in the day, they would talk to each other on the phone twice a day except for the two weeks a year when the Browns and Steelers would play. Then they didn't talk. My mom instilled in me a sense of loyalty based on that. She never understood her sister changing allegiances and she always said you stick with your teams because they represent your city. I never thought there would be a time when I would feel such animosity toward the Browns. But Deshaun Watson definitely made me feel that way. Ineptitude and losing I can live with. Holding up someone who preyed on women as a role model, I can't abide. Still there always will be a part of me that loves the Browns.

— Nancy Sommer, Cleveland, Ohio

Friends make fun of me for following the Browns, especially here in Maryland. My family tells me my favorite color is "Disappointment Brown."

— Dan Clawson, Bel Air, Maryland

I swear off the Browns after every loss! But I know it's just a 24-hour thing. I'll be back.

— Lee Long, Stow, Ohio

ACKNOWLEDGMENTS

There always are people to thank with any book project, but I'm starting with you—my readers. It's very simple . . . no readers, no book. Without you, I'd have had to find a real job for the last 50 years.

That also applies to a publisher. No publisher, no book.

Yes, you can self-publish books now, but it's not something I'd want to try. With each passing year, I need more help with writing stories and especially books. That's why I am so grateful to David Gray, who has been my publisher since 2000. In the same span that he has published 17 of my books, the Browns have had 40 quarterbacks. If only the Browns could have found their David Gray to be the quarterback . . .

In terms of help, Larry Pantages has been my researcher and partner in shaping this book. It's our fourth project together. But Larry and I go back to . . . 1985! That's when I replaced him as the Cavs beat writer at the Akron Beacon Journal. He moved to the Business News department as he wanted to get off the road and raise his family. Larry later was my sports editor at the Akron Beacon Journal.

Thanks to Skip Hall. If only the Browns had someone like him to prevent them from making mistakes, they'd be in much better shape today.

Faith Hamlin has been my agent since . . . well, a long time . . . at least 40 years. I'm really grateful to her as she has supported me when I moved back and forth from sports to faith writing.

David Campbell is a tremendous sports editor and friend at cleveland.com/The Plain Dealer. Along with cleveland.com editor Chris Quinn, he has been very supportive of not only my writing for the website and paper, but also my books.

Roberta and I have been married 48 years and in that span, we've done more than 30 books together. We've lost count. Roberta has been there for each one, giving them the first read, checking facts and fixing my grammar, etc. If the Browns had scouted, drafted and signed free agents as well as I did finding Roberta . . . then I'd have been writing books about them being a Super Bowl power.

ABOUT THE AUTHOR

Terry Pluto is the author of more than 30 books. He won the National Headliner Award as the nation's best sports columnist in 2020 and was the runner-up in 2022. His degree from Cleveland State is in secondary education. He taught social studies for six months at Lincoln-West High to become state certified. He has spent 66 of his 70 years in Northeast Ohio and loves writing for the local fans. He has been married to Roberta for 48 years, and she has been a partner in all of his book projects. He has been a sports and faith columnist for cleveland.com / The Plain Dealer since 2007.

OTHER BOOKS BY TERRY PLUTO . . .

Vintage Browns

A Warm Look Back at the Cleveland Browns of the 1970s, '80s, '90s and More

Terry Pluto

Like a classic throwback jersey, this book recalls favorite players and moments from Cleveland Browns teams of the 1970s, '80s, '90s and more. Visit with Bernie Kosar, Ozzie Newsome, Brian Sipe, Marty Schottenheimer, Doug Dieken, Kevin Mack, Bill Belichik and others from days when the "Kardiac Kids" and the "Dawgs" ruled the old Stadium.

The Browns Blues

Two Decades of Utter Frustration: Why Everything Kept Going Wrong for the Cleveland Browns

Terry Pluto

How could things go so wrong for so long? From their return in 1999 through the winless 2017 season, the Cleveland Browns had the worst record in the NFL. And their fans had ulcers. Veteran sports columnist Terry Pluto explains two decades of front-office upheaval and frustrating football in this detailed, behind-the-scenes analysis.

Browns Town 1964

The Cleveland Browns and the 1964 Championship

Terry Pluto

A nostalgic look back at the upstart AFC Cleveland Browns' surprising 1964 championship victory over the hugely favored Baltimore Colts. Profiles the colorful players who made that season memorable, including Jim Brown, Paul Warfield, Frank Ryan. Recreates an era and a team for which pride was not just a slogan.

"Pluto movingly reveals the substance of a mythic bond between men and a game, a team and a city—and thus lays bare how present-day pro football has surrendered its soul." – Kirkus Reviews

OTHER BOOKS BY TERRY PLUTO . . .

Things I've Learned from Watching the Browns

Terry Pluto

Veteran sports writer Terry Pluto asks Cleveland Browns fans: Why, after four decades of heartbreak, teasing, and futility, do you still stick with this team? Their stories, coupled with Pluto's own insight and analysis, deliver the answers. Like any intense relationship, it's complicated. But these fans just won't give up.

"For dedicated Browns fans [the book is] like leafing through an old family photo album." – BlogCritics.com

False Start

How the New Browns Were Set Up to Fail

Terry Pluto

A hard look at the unhappy beginnings of the post-1999 Cleveland Browns franchise, this book chronicles the backroom deals, big-money power plays, poor decisions, and plain bad luck that dogged the venerable franchise after Art Modell skipped town in 1995. How long should fans have to wait for a winner? A book the NFL does not want you to read.

"A fascinating, behind-the-scenes look at how the new Browns were created and what's kept them from making the progress everyone expected." – Houston Chronicle

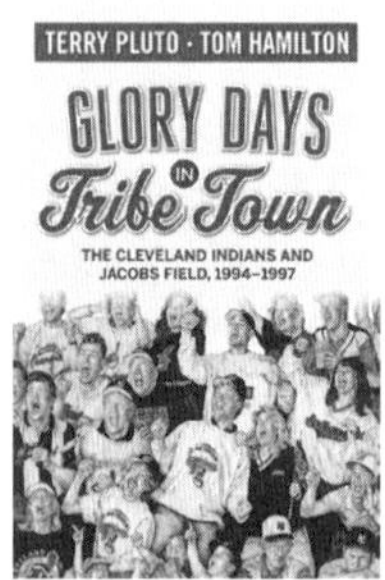

Glory Days in Tribe Town

The Cleveland Indians and Jacobs Field 1994–1997

Terry Pluto, Tom Hamilton

Relive the most thrilling seasons of Indians baseball in recent memory! Cleveland's top sportswriter teams up with the Tribe's veteran radio announcer and fans to share favorite stories from the first years of Jacobs Field, when a star-studded roster (Belle, Thome, Vizquel, Ramirez, Alomar, Nagy) and a sparkling ballpark captivated an entire city.

More at **www.grayco.com**

OTHER BOOKS BY TERRY PLUTO . . .

Our Tribe

A Baseball Memoir

Terry Pluto

A son, a father, a baseball team. Sportswriter Terry Pluto's memoir tells about growing up and learning to understand a difficult father through their shared love of an often awful baseball team. Baseball can be an important bridge across generations, sometimes the only common ground. This story celebrates the connection.

"A beautiful, absolutely unforgettable memoir." – Booklist

The Curse of Rocky Colavito

A Loving Look at a Thirty-Year Slump

Terry Pluto

A baseball classic. No sports fans suffered more miserable teams for more seasons than Indians fans of the 1960s, '70s, and '80s. Here's a fond and often humorous look back at "the bad old days" of the Tribe. The definitive book about the Indians of that generation, and a great piece of sports history writing.

"The year's funniest and most insightful baseball book." – Chicago Tribune

Vintage Cavs

A Warm Look Back at the Cavaliers of the Cleveland Arena and Richfield Coliseum Years

Terry Pluto

The Cleveland Arena and Richfield Coliseum are long gone, but they and the Cavaliers teams from 1970 to the 1990s come alive in this personal history by a sportswriter who was there as a young fan and later an NBA beat writer. From expansion team to the brink of greatness with Austin Carr, World B. Free, "Hot Rod" Williams, Mark Price, and others.

More at **www.grayco.com**

OTHER BOOKS BY TERRY PLUTO . . .

Joe Tait: It's Been a Real Ball

Stories from a Hall-of-Fame Sports Broadcasting Career

Terry Pluto, Joe Tait

Legendary broadcaster Joe Tait is like an old family friend to three generations of Cleveland sports fans. This book celebrates the inspiring career of "the Voice of the Cleveland Cavaliers" with stories from Joe and dozens of fans, colleagues, and players. Hits the highlights of a long career and also uncovers some touching personal details.

"An easy, fun book to read and will surely bring back good memories for Cleveland sports fans who listened to Tait's trademark calls since 1970." – 20SecondTimeout.com

The Comeback: LeBron, the Cavs & Cleveland

How LeBron James Came Home and Brought a Championship to Cleveland

Terry Pluto

One of the greatest Cleveland sports stories ever! In this epic homecoming tale, LeBron James and the Cavaliers take fans on a roller coaster ride from despair to hope and, finally, to glory as the 2016 NBA champions. Terry Pluto tells how it all happened, with insightful analysis and behind-the-scenes details.

The Franchise

LeBron James and the Remaking of the Cleveland Cavaliers

Terry Pluto, Brian Windhorst

An in-depth look at how a team and a city were rebuilt around LeBron James. Two award-winning sports journalists tell the converging stories of a struggling franchise and a hometown teenage phenom. Will fascinate basketball fans who want the inside story of a young superstar shouldering the weight of an entire NBA franchise.

"Not your typical sports biography . . . Take[s] the reader behind the scenes in the Cavaliers' front office, revealing how championship contenders are built" – Library Journal

More at **www.grayco.com**